AMERICAN
WAR LIBRARY
★ ★ ★ ★

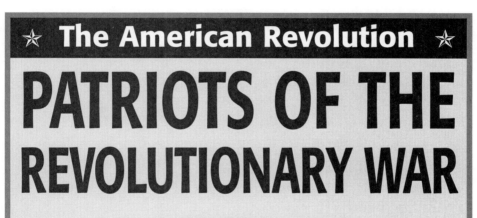

★ The American Revolution ★

PATRIOTS OF THE REVOLUTIONARY WAR

by Charles Clark

Titles in The American War Library series include:

AMERICAN WAR LIBRARY

★ ★ ★ ★

★ The American Revolution ★

PATRIOTS OF THE REVOLUTIONARY WAR

by Charles Clark

LUCENT
BOOKS®

THOMSON

GALE

San Diego • Detroit • New York • San Francisco • Cleveland • New Haven, Conn. • Waterville, Maine • London • Munich

© 2003 by Lucent Books. Lucent Books is an imprint of The Gale Group, Inc.,
a division of Thomson Learning, Inc.

Lucent Books® and Thomson Learning™ are trademarks used herein under license.

For more information, contact
Lucent Books
27500 Drake Rd.
Farmington Hills, MI 48331-3535
Or you can visit our Internet site at http://www.gale.com

LIBRARY OF CONGRESS CATALOGING-IN-PUBLICATION DATA

Clark, Charles, 1949–
    Patriots of the Revolutionary War / by Charles Clark.
        p. cm. — (American war library. The American Revolution series)
Summary: Profiles five American patriots, looking especially at their service as
soldiers and/or diplomats during the Revolutionary War.
Includes bibliographical references and index.
        ISBN 1-59018-220-0 (alk. paper)
        1. United States—History—Revolution, 1775–1783—Biography—Juvenile
literature.   [1. United States—History—Revolution, 1775–1783—Biography.]
I. Title.   II. American war library. American Revolution series.
        E206 .C54 2003
        973.3'092'2—dc21
                                                                2002011030

Printed in the United States of America

★ Contents ★

A Nation Forged by War

The United States, like many nations, was forged and defined by war. Despite Benjamin Franklin's opinion that "There never was a good war or a bad peace," the United States owes its very existence to the War of Independence, one to which Franklin wholeheartedly subscribed. The country forged by war in 1776 was tempered and made stronger by the Civil War in the 1860s.

The Texas Revolution, the Mexican-American War, and the Spanish-American War expanded the country's borders and gave it overseas possessions. These wars made the United States a world power, but this status came with a price, as the nation became a key but reluctant player in both World War I and World War II.

Each successive war further defined the country's role on the world stage. Following World War II, U.S. foreign policy redefined itself to focus on the role of defender, not only of the freedom of its own citizens, but also of the freedom of people everywhere. During the cold war that followed World War II until the collapse of the Soviet Union, defending the world meant fighting communism. This goal, manifested in the Korean and Vietnam conflicts, proved elusive, and soured the American public on its achievability. As the United States emerged as the world's sole superpower, American foreign policy has been guided less by national interest and more on protecting international human rights. But as involvement in Somalia and Kosovo proves, this goal has been equally elusive.

As a result, the country's view of itself changed. Bolstered by victories in World Wars I and II, Americans first relished the role of protector. But, as war followed war in a seemingly endless procession, Americans began to doubt their leaders, their motives, and themselves. The Vietnam War especially caused people to question the validity of sending its young people to die in places where they were not particularly wanted and for people who did not seem especially grateful.

While the most obvious changes brought about by America's wars have been geopolitical in nature, many other aspects of society have been touched. War often does not bring about change directly, but acts instead like the catalyst in a chemical reaction, accelerating changes already in progress.

Some of these changes have been societal. The role of women in the United States had been slowly changing, but World War II put thousands into the workforce and into uniform. They might have gone back to being housewives after the war, but equality, once experienced, would not be forgotten.

Likewise, wars have accelerated technological change. The necessity for faster airplanes and a more destructive bomb led to the development of jet planes and nuclear energy. Artificial fibers developed for parachutes in the 1940s were used in the clothing of the 1950s.

Lucent Books' American War Library covers key wars in the development of the nation. Each war is covered in several volumes, to allow for more detail, context, and to provide volumes on often neglected subjects, such as the kamikazes of World War II, or weapons used in the Civil War. As with all Lucent Books, notes, annotated bibliographies, and appendixes such as glossaries give students a launching point for further research. In addition, sidebars and archival photographs enhance the text. Together, each volume in The American War Library will aid students in understanding how America's wars have shaped and changed its politics, economics, and society.

Five Leaders

Before the First Continental Congress met in Philadelphia in 1774, Boston lawyer John Adams worried about the chances of its success because, he thought, there were so few men capable of meeting the challenges the American colonies faced in their dispute with Great Britain. Adams wrote in his diary, "We have not men fit for the times. . . . We are deficient in genius, in education, in travel, in fortune—in everything."[1]

After the Congress convened, however, and Adams had seen his fellow delegates at work, his opinion changed. Then he wrote in his diary that the members had "fortunes, abilities, learning, eloquence, [and] acuteness" more than equal to the task. In a letter to his wife Abigail, Adams wrote, "This assembly is like no other that ever existed. Every man in it is a great man—an orator, a critic, a statesman."[2]

History has agreed with Adams's judgment. The American Revolution could not have happened the way that it did and with so good a result without the extraordinary talents of its leaders. The Revolution had many sorts of leaders who played various roles. Some raised the money needed to fund the army. Some worked out the relations of the new United States with other nations. Some led troops in battle. Some worked behind the battle lines to keep the wheels of the Revolution turning.

The people who began the Revolution were British subjects, but it seemed to many of them that they were being treated unfairly by the British government. At first, many American patriots only wanted equitable treatment, expecting that once the British government saw the error of its ways the American colonies would not only stay in the British Empire but become even more closely tied to it. Benjamin Franklin was one of those who wanted reconciliation with Britain, although he foresaw a day when

British America would surpass the mother country in population and wealth.

American patriots knew the American colonies were in a unique and confusing situation. They were British subjects, but they were not allowed to elect members to the British Parliament. Many Americans, therefore, thought that although the colonial legislatures were empowered to raise money through taxes, Parliament did not have the right to impose taxes on the colonies. This is the origin of the famous rallying cry, "No taxation without representation!"

To the surprise of American patriots, their complaints about taxes produced hostile reactions from the British, and in 1763 a series of crises began that led to the outbreak of significant fighting between the king's troops and the colonial militias in 1775. Thus, by the mid-1770s it was clear to most patriots that some kind of independence was needed. The first concrete step in that direction happened a year and a day before the Declaration of Independence, when on July 3,

1775, George Washington, a Virginian, took command of an army made up of militias from several colonies to force the British out of Boston. This was the first time the colonies had done more than talk about unity.

The Declaration of Independence is read to Washington's army in 1776.

In the year after Washington took command, colonial troops fought the British in Canada, captured some of their cannons, and used them to force the redcoats out of Boston. Meeting in Philadelphia, in July 1776 the Continental Congress agreed to endorse a document drafted by Thomas Jefferson—the Declaration of Independence—that stated the resolve of the colonies to unite and to be independent from Britain.

Another five years of war followed. The British were forced to withdraw their claims to the colonies, but this did not resolve the question of what sort of nation the United States would become. Just how would the states be united? Only in matters of war? What about commerce? Would laws apply to all the states? If so, who would enforce them? How would the nation resolve disputes between states? It would take many more years to resolve these issues.

The subjects of this book were all important figures in the Revolution. All of them participated in the war, though not all as soldiers. Benjamin Franklin had been a world-famous scientist, writer, and patriot for many years before the war. John Adams and Thomas Jefferson had played crucial roles in many of the decisions leading up to the war, but they were not soldiers—their contribution to the war itself was political and diplomatic. Paul Revere was deeply involved in prerevolutionary activities in Boston and in the war itself. Alexander Hamilton served in the army during the war, both as a field commander and as Washington's assistant, and went on to important roles in the ratification of the Constitution and a controversial term as secretary of the treasury.

Many historians have contended that the American Revolution had no clear beginning and no clear ending. The patriots discussed here demonstrate that point. They gradually became more involved in the Revolutionary movement, rose to positions of importance, and—often despite their best efforts to retire to private life—spent the rest of their days as part of the vast enterprise of working out what sort of nation the United States of America would become.

Chapter 1

Benjamin Franklin

Benjamin Franklin was a central figure in the American Revolution, participating in the most important events of the era. He was the only person to sign each of three very important documents: the Declaration of Independence, the Treaty of Paris ending the Revolutionary War, and the Constitution. As ambassador to France during the war, Franklin persuaded the French to give much-needed aid to the rebels.

As a young man, Franklin was ambitious and enterprising, and he soon found great success as a printer, writer, and publisher. Franklin's annual *Poor Richard's Almanac* was among the most widely read publications in America, and the sharp political satires he published in newspapers and magazines in America and England made him a popular and effective advocate for American rights.

In the years after the Revolution, Americans regarded Franklin as second only to George Washington among the founders of the nation, and historians today generally agree with that opinion. His effectiveness as a leader grew from the reputation he had earned before the war, both in the American colonies and in Europe, as a writer, scientist, and political thinker. Among Europeans, he was the best-known and most respected American before the war, and his status meant that he was taken seriously by European kings and politicians.

Childhood

Benjamin Franklin was born in Boston, Massachusetts, on January 17, 1706, into a large family—he was the tenth and youngest son and the fifteenth of seventeen children. His father, Josiah Franklin, had come to Boston from England around 1682 because his church, known as the Conventicles, had been outlawed. Josiah was a tallow-chandler, meaning that he processed the fat of cattle and sheep into tallow, which was used to make candles and soap. Josiah had seven children with his first wife and ten with his second. Though not wealthy, Josiah was highly respected among Boston merchants, who often sought his advice.

When Benjamin Franklin was eight he was enrolled in a grammar school, which was intended for those going on to college. He quickly proved to be the best pupil in the school. But after a few months his father decided the family would not be able to afford to send Franklin to college, so the next year he was sent instead to a school that taught writing and arithmetic.

At age ten he left school to help in the tallow shop. Franklin did not like tallow making, however. His father feared that he might go to sea, as one of his brothers had, so when Benjamin was twelve his father apprenticed him to Benjamin's older brother James, who had a printing shop in Boston. Franklin was to remain an apprentice until he was twenty-one. This was about two years longer than apprenticeships usually lasted, and it proved to be much too long for Franklin.

Benjamin Franklin's early introduction to printing and publishing allowed him to cultivate his skills as a writer and thinker.

Reader and Writer

Franklin learned the printing trade quickly, but his real interests lay elsewhere. He was a great reader, beginning when he was very young. In his *Autobiography,* he said that he could not remember a time when he could not read. Books were among his most prized possessions, and he often asked people to lend him books. Because he knew other apprentices who worked for booksellers, he was able to borrow books at closing time, read late into the night, and then return the books when the bookshop opened the next morning.

Franklin's writing career began when he was still a teenager. With his brother's encouragement he wrote two poems, one about a shipwreck and the other about the pirate Blackbeard. He printed them and sold them on the street. Even though he made a profit, his father convinced him that he was not a very good poet and that poets were generally poor. Franklin agreed, but he decided that writing would be a useful skill to master. In 1722 he published his first newspaper articles, an anonymous series of satires that he wrote under the pen name of Silence Dogood. These appeared in his brother's paper, the *New-England Courant*. Even his brother did not know who had written them, and Franklin took great pleasure in listening to James and others discuss them approvingly.

As a teenager, Franklin's relationship with his brother James was often strained. Franklin was exceptionally bright, knowledgeable, and inventive, and he wanted to put his good ideas into action. In his position as an apprentice, though, he was expected to follow orders, not initiate grand schemes. By accident, Benjamin got his chance to show what he could do.

James's newspaper published a story that angered the colonial Assembly, which issued an order for James's arrest and prohibited him from publishing the *Courant*. To evade the order, James went into hiding and named the seventeen-year-old Benjamin as publisher. Benjamin remained the publisher of record for several months.

Philadelphia

Benjamin was brilliant, ambitious, and eager to demonstrate his talents and to establish his independence. James probably just wanted an obedient apprentice, and he may have been jealous of a younger brother who was obviously more clever than he was. Exactly what disagreements arose between Benjamin and James is uncertain, but they apparently had frequent arguments, and James sometimes beat Benjamin.

Benjamin decided to quit. Normally, he could have been arrested for quitting because he had legally obligated himself to work for James until he was twenty-one. But Benjamin had a way out: When James named him publisher of the *Courant*, he also had to release him from his indentures, or appear to. James signed the release, but he and Benjamin then made out a secret indenture saying that Benjamin would stay on. This secret indenture was illegal and so not enforceable. Benjamin reasoned that he was justified in leaving James because of the beatings, but in later years he thought this

might have been a mistake. In his *Autobiography* he wrote,

Indentured to his brother James, Franklin (pictured) toiled unhappily as an apprentice printer.

I took upon me to assert my Freedom, presuming that he [James] would not venture to produce the new Indentures. It was not fair of me to take this Advantage, and this I therefore reckon one of the first Errata [mistakes] of my Life: But the Unfairness of it weigh'd little with me, when under the Impressions of Resentment, for the Blows his Passion too often urg'd him to bestow upon me. Tho' He was otherwise not an ill-natur'd Man: Perhaps I was too saucy and provoking.[3]

When Franklin announced that he was going to leave his apprenticeship, James convinced the other printers in Boston not to hire him. Franklin left Boston secretly and sought work first in New York and then in Philadelphia. There, Franklin soon had a job as a printer. In fact, he discovered that he was the most skilled printer in Philadelphia, the two shop owners of the time having little training or experience in the trade.

Franklin quickly developed a wide range of friends in his adopted city. He lodged at the home of John Read, a building contractor. Franklin especially liked living with the Reads because of their pretty young daughter Deborah. Through his brother-in-law, ship captain Robert Homes, Franklin was introduced to the governor of Pennsylvania, Sir William Keith, who was immediately impressed with the young man. Keith complained that the quality of printing available in Philadelphia was deplorable and proposed to set Franklin up in business, even offering to send him to London to get the necessary equipment.

Franklin's father thought Benjamin was too young to have his own shop, but the governor insisted. Franklin kept the plan secret in Philadelphia, which proved to be a mistake. Those who knew the governor were aware that he made extravagant promises that he was unable to keep. Franklin only learned when he reached England that Governor Keith had not provided the letters of credit and intro-

A Life Well Lived

Franklin wanted his family and others to benefit from what he had learned in his long life of invention, accomplishment, and reflection. In his *Autobiography* he wrote:

> Having emerg'd from the Poverty & Obscurity in which I was born & bred, to a state of Affluence & some Degree of Reputation in the World, and having gone so far thro' life with a considerable Share of Felicity [happiness] . . . my Posterity may like to know, as they may find some of them suitable to their own Situations, & therefore fit to be imitated.—That Felicity, when I reflected on it, has induc'd me sometimes to say, that were it offer'd to my Choice, I should have no Objection to a Repetition of the same Life from its Beginning, only asking the Advantages Authors have in a second Edition to correct some Faults of the first.

duction that Franklin needed to carry out the plan.

Franklin was only briefly dismayed. Though three thousand miles from home and virtually penniless, Franklin quickly found work with a London printer and stayed in England a year and a half, returning when he was offered a job by a Philadelphia businessman, Thomas Denham. Franklin was then only nineteen years old.

Return to Philadelphia

Franklin opened a store with Denham, but Denham soon died. Franklin went back to work for the printer who had first employed him, Samuel Keimer, but this time Franklin was made manager of the print shop. For a while, things went smoothly. Franklin later wrote that the other workers

> all respected me, the more as they found Keimer incapable of instructing them, and that from me they learnt something daily. We never worked on a Saturday, that being Keimer's Sabbath. So I had two days for reading. My acquaintance with ingenious people in the town, increased. Keimer himself treated me with great civility, and apparent regard.[4]

Franklin suspected, however, that Keimer might fire him as soon as the shop was running smoothly, and in fact Keimer did so. Again unemployed, Franklin soon arranged to set up a printing shop with a fellow apprentice in Keimer's shop, Hugh Meredith, with financial help from Meredith's father. As in his plan with Governor Keith, it would take several months to get the equipment from England.

It was not long before Franklin found a way to support himself while waiting for his printing press. Keimer got a contract to print money for New Jersey (each colony had its own currency), but he knew he could not complete the job without Franklin's help. He apologized to Franklin and asked him to come back to work. Franklin agreed. This gave Franklin both an income and a way to train Hugh, his secret partner, at Keimer's expense.

But business was not all that occupied Franklin's attention.

Marriage

Though he no longer lived with them, Franklin maintained contact with the Read family, and his affection for Deborah continued to grow. While Franklin was in England, Deborah Read had married a potter named Rogers, but she soon left him. Rogers was rumored to have already been married and to have died in the West Indies, though neither the prior marriage nor the death could be proved. Franklin wrote, "We ventured, however, over all these Difficulties, and I took her to Wife Sept. 1, 1730."[5] There was no ceremony or legal record of the marriage—marriages were often entered into and dissolved without ceremony in those days. One reason they did not record the marriage may have been that new husbands could be held responsible for the debts of a previous husband, but an even greater deterrent was the penalty for bigamy: thirty-nine lashes and life in prison.

The Young Philosopher of Self-Improvement

Franklin found that Deborah was a good housekeeper—she took care of things and let him pursue his many interests and projects, among them developing a personal philosophy. Though never an active member of a church, Franklin was convinced that religion was good for the community. He contributed to the building

Deborah Read married Benjamin Franklin in 1730.

ing to house his Philadelphia meetings, Franklin raised the money to build a hall for the use of any preacher, regardless of denomination. Franklin later boasted that "even if the Mufti of Constantinople were to send a Missionary to preach [Islam] to us, he would find a Pulpit at his Service."[6]

Because Franklin had no church to guide him in improving his character, he drew up his own list of virtues: temperance, silence, order, resolution, frugality, industry, sincerity, justice, moderation, cleanliness, tranquility, chastity, and humility. He developed an elaborate system to help him practice these virtues and keep track of how well he did. He eventually gave up using the system, but his attempts at self-improvement would continue in different forms for the rest of his life.

Citizen Franklin

Franklin not only wanted to improve himself; he also wanted to help others and to improve his city. Though he was busy in his printing shop, he still found time for a wide range of other projects. Like his

funds of many churches and attended the sermons of traveling preachers. He was especially attracted to the English evangelist George Whitefield, who became a close friend. Franklin published Whitefield's journals and sermons, and when Whitefield could not find a build-work of building a lecture hall for visiting preachers, when Franklin saw a need, he did his best to fill it. For example, Franklin thought he and others would benefit from reading and discussing books on science, politics, and ethics, so he formed a club known as the Junto. Franklin wrote the rules for the Junto, which "requir'd that every Member . . . once in three months produce and read an Essay of his own Writing on any Subject he pleased. Our Debates were to be . . . conducted in the sincere Spirit of Enquiry after Truth, without fondness for Dispute, or Desire for victory."[7]

The Junto became a springboard for other projects. One of these was the Library Company of Philadelphia. For a time the Junto had a common library for its members. Seeing how helpful this was, Franklin proposed and organized a subscription library open to anyone. Members paid an initial fee, which went into a fund to buy the basic collection of books, and then an annual subscription fee. They could borrow one book at a time, signing a promissory note for twice the value of the book in the event it was lost. In his *Autobiography*, Franklin wrote:

The Institution soon manifested its Utility, was imitated by other Towns and in other Provinces. . . . Reading became fashionable, and our People, having no publick Amusements to divert their Attention from Study became better acquainted with Books, and in a few Years were observ'd by Strangers to be better instructed & more intelligent than People of the same Rank generally are in other Countries.[8]

English evangelist George Whitefield gestures during a sermon. Whitefield's sermons and journals were published by Franklin.

The Junto itself provided at least a partial model for one of Franklin's most enduring projects, a fellowship of scientists to be called the American Philosophical Society. ("Philosophy" referred to natural philosophy, what is today called science.) Though the idea had been discussed before, Franklin wrote and published a proposal and then corresponded with potential members and supporters. The American Philosophical Society became one of the most important scientific institutions in the early days of the United States. It still operates today from its headquarters in Philadelphia.

Franklin also founded a hospital, a system of fire brigades, and a militia company, and he reorganized the colonial postal system, cutting delivery times in half. A school he established later became the University of Pennsylvania. Franklin seemed capable of taking on almost any project, either in his business or in his civic life.

A Man of Means and Influence

Franklin was very good at innovation and organization, but he quickly tired of managing the enterprises he founded. One of the endeavors he worked at the longest, though, was *Poor Richard's Almanac,* his annual book of astronomical tables, weather predictions, humor, and wisdom that became one of the most popular series in colonial America.

By the time he was forty-two years old, Franklin's businesses produced enough income to allow him to devote himself to his scientific, philosophical, and civic interests. Franklin was not interested in money for its own sake. He thought the only good thing about money was that it could buy him the time to pursue interesting and useful projects.

In 1754 Franklin's renown as author and publisher of *Poor Richard's Almanac* and as a civic leader in Philadelphia led to his first involvement in the question of the relationship of the American colonies to Great Britain. A war between Britain and France was imminent, and so the colonies were asked to send delegates to a conference with leaders of the Iroquois Nation, which was allied with Britain, to develop a plan for their common defense.

What emerged was a plan, drafted by Franklin, not only for defense of the colonies but also for their union. The plan raised issues that were crucial in the conflicts and debates that dominated the next two decades. The disputes that led to the Revolution centered on the powers and responsibilities of the king, Parliament, and the colonial assemblies. Franklin's plan clarified these issues. It proposed a president-general to be selected by Britain and a Grand Council composed of representatives of each of the colonies. This would turn the separate colonies into a single political entity, at least for some purposes, and make them even more closely related to Britain.

The colonies thought Franklin's plan gave too much power to the president-general because he would have a veto over

Poor Richard, 1733.

AN

Almanack

For the Year of Chrift

1733,

Being the Firft after LEAP YEAR:

And makes fince the Creation	Years
By the Account of the Eastern *Greeks*	7241
By the Latin Church, when ☉ ent. ♈	6932
By the Computation of *W. W.*	5742
By the *Roman* Chronology	5682
By the *Jewish* Rabbies	5494

Wherein is contained

The Lunations, Eclipfes, Judgment of the Weather, Spring Tides, Planets Motions & mutual Afpects, Sun and Moon's Rifing and Setting, Length of Days, Time of High Water, Fairs, Courts, and obfervable Days.

Fitted to the Latitude of Forty Degrees, and a Meridian of Five Hours Weft from *London*, but may without fenfible Error, ferve all the adjacent Places, even from *Newfoundland* to *South-Carolina*.

By *RICHARD SAUNDERS*, Philom.

PHILADELPHIA:

Printed and fold by *B. FRANKLIN*, at the New Printing-Office near the Market.

Franklin's annual Poor Richard's Almanac *was one of the most popular books in colonial America.*

give the colonists a voice in their government, especially taxation. He realized that even though the Grand Council might not improve the efficiency of government, it would make a big psychological difference for the colonists. He wrote, "Where heavy burthens have been laid on them, it has been found useful to make it, as much as possible, their own act; for they bear better when they have, or think they have some share in the direction."[9]

Advocate for Freedom

In 1757 Franklin was named the Pennsylvania colony's agent to England, meaning that he would represent the colony's interests to the mother country. He sailed for London in June, found lodgings in London, and quickly became a popular figure in Britain. He had many friends in London and other parts of Britain, and he liked living there. He was generally successful in his work as colonial agent, he participated actively in scientific societies, and he was awarded honorary degrees by two universities. He returned to America in 1762, and he was active in Pennsylvania politics for two years before being sent back to London, again as colonial agent.

In 1765 and 1766 Franklin had a central role in one of the controversies that set the stage for the Revolution. Britain wanted to tax the colonies and passed a law called the Stamp Act, which

laws passed by the council. Despite this veto power, the British thought the plan was too democratic. Franklin wanted to

required that all newspapers and legal documents in the colonies have stamps attached to them, which had to be bought from British agents. The law sparked protests throughout the colonies. Franklin testified in the House of Commons against the law, calling it unfair. He declared that the colonies could not afford to pay the tax, and that opposition to it was so great that armed rebellion was likely. Franklin's speech was credited with turning the tide in favor of repeal. But on the same day, Parliament passed the Declaratory Act, which reaffirmed Parliament's right to tax the colonies.

Franklin was becoming more convinced that Britain and America would not find a way to maintain their connection. He saw inevitable problems, and his vision of the coming conflict was remarkably accurate. In an April 1767 letter to the Scottish judge Lord Kames—over nine years before the Declaration of Independence—Franklin foresaw much that would happen in the coming years:

America, an immense territory, favoured by nature with all advantages of climate, soil, great navigable rivers, and lakes, etc. must become a great country, populous and mighty; and will, in a less time than is generally conceived, be able to shake off any shackles that may be imposed on her [by Britain], and perhaps place them on the imposers. In the meantime, every act of oppression will sour their

Adams on Franklin

In the early days of the Revolution, some people questioned Franklin's allegiance to America because he had lived in England so long and was close to many loyalists, including his son, who was royal governor of New Jersey. John Adams, however, wrote to his wife that in the Second Continental Congress Franklin showed himself to be a patriot. (The letter is found in *The Book of Abigail and John: Selected Letters of the Adams Family*.)

Dr. Franklin has been very constant in his Attendance on Congress from the Beginning. His Conduct has been composed and grave and in the Opinion of many Gentlemen very reserved. He has not assumed any Thing, nor affected to take the lead; . . . Yet he has not been backward: has been very usefull, on many occasions, and discovered [shown] a Disposition entirely American. He does not hesitate at our boldest Measures, but rather seems to think us, too irresolute, and backward. He thinks us at present in an odd State, neither in Peace nor War, neither dependent nor independent. . . .

He thinks, that We have the Power of preserving ourselves, and that even if We should be driven to the disagreeable Necessity of assuming a total independency, and set up a separate state, We could maintain it. . . . He is . . . a great and good Man.

tempers, lessen greatly, if not annihilate the profits of your commerce with them, and hasten their final revolt.[10]

The esteem in which Franklin was held by the colonies continued to grow. By 1771 Franklin was agent to Britain not only for Pennsylvania but also for New Jersey, Georgia, and Massachusetts.

The Hutchinson Letters

In December 1772 Franklin obtained letters that Thomas Hutchinson, the royal governor of Massachusetts, and Andrew Oliver, Hutchinson's brother-in-law, had written to British officials urging them to use harsh measures against the colonists. Franklin forwarded the letters to Thomas Cushing, speaker of the Massachusetts House, to show that the new taxes and other laws were the fault of the colonial administration, not of the king and his ministers.

Franklin still preferred a reconciliation between the colonies and England. He had lived in England for nearly fifteen years and felt at home there. While he was committed to American liberty, he thought that was best achieved by having the colonists treated in exactly the same way that other British subjects were, and by a union of the colonies with Britain that would create a single imperial commonwealth. Franklin felt that if this were done, the united empire would be invincible. But despite this, Franklin was called before a committee of Parliament and severely criticized for his role in making the Hutchinson letters public. Though for a time he was in danger of being arrested, no formal charges were ever brought.

The Gathering Storm

In the worsening relationship between Britain and the colonies, controversy swirled around Franklin. He was the best-known and most effective of the colonial agents and so a frequent target of critics, but he stayed on in London so that he could represent the views of the colonies directly to those in power. Parliament declared Massachusetts to be in rebellion in February 1775, and about the same time Franklin heard that his wife Deborah had died two months earlier in Philadelphia. He left England in March and arrived home in May.

Franklin was selected to serve in the Second Continental Congress, an assembly of delegates from the colonies that would consider what to do about the crisis, and in June 1776 he was named to the committee to draft the Declaration of Independence. Though his contributions to the document were slight, his support for the decision to break with Britain was important. The delegates knew Franklin loved England; his belief that independence was necessary helped to convince the undecided.

One of the personal tragedies of the Revolution for Franklin concerned his son William, who was the royal governor of New Jersey. The two had been close in quieter times, and the first part of Franklin's *Autobiography* is proudly addressed to his distinguished son. But William decided to remain loyal to Britain. When William was arrested by Continental authorities at the beginning of the war, Franklin refused to intervene on his behalf. William was freed in 1778

Members of the Second Continental Congress prepare to sign the Declaration of Independence in 1776.

in a prisoner exchange and participated in the war against America. He later moved to England, where he was given a government pension. Franklin regarded William's allegiance to Britain as a personal betrayal and seemed never to fully forgive him.

Diplomat

In September 1776 Franklin was selected to be one of the representatives of the new United States in France. The American relationship with France was crucial. France and Britain were long-standing and bitter enemies, so France was eager to help America break away from Britain.

Franklin's job, which he shared with others appointed by Congress, was to convince the French to give as much as possible in money, arms, and troops. Franklin reached Paris in December 1776, and in January the French king promised a substantial loan to the United States.

Franklin was over seventy years old during his time in Paris and wanted to enjoy his life as well as conduct diplomacy. He had a huge range of friends and admirers with whom he spent much of each day, and this caused many disagreements with his fellow commissioners. Though Franklin's extensive social contacts helped in diplomacy, the other commissioners complained to Congress about the difficulty they had getting Franklin to attend to business.

To make relations more harmonious and to safeguard the progress of negotiations, Congress made Franklin sole ambassador in September 1778. He accomplished a great deal as ambassador: He negotiated more loans, bought arms and

Life in Paris

In a letter that can be found in Esmond Wright's book *Benjamin Franklin: His Life as He Wrote It*, Franklin told his sister Jane Mecom about his life in Paris:

> I enjoy here an exceeding good state of health, I live in a fine airy house upon a hill, which has a large garden with fine walks in it, about half an hour's drive [in a horse-drawn carriage] from the city of Paris. I walk a little every day in the garden, have a good appetite and sleep well. I think the French cookery agrees with me better than the English; I suppose because there is little or no butter in their sauces; for I have never once had the heartburn since my being here though I eat heartily, which shows that my digestion is good. I have got into a good neighbourhood, of a very agreeable people who appear very fond of me; at least they are pleasingly civil: so that upon the whole I live as comfortably as a man can well do so far from his home and family.

material for the Continental army, managed the affairs of the navy abroad, and obtained French letters of marque for American privateers. (Letters of marque allowed private vessels to capture enemy ships under government auspices.) His best-known effort in this period was in gaining French support for the American navy officer John Paul Jones, who was so grateful that he renamed his flagship the *Bonhomme Richard* (Poor Richard).

The Treaty of Paris, which formally ended the Revolutionary War, was one of Franklin's greatest accomplishments. Beginning in 1781, Franklin managed the complex and sensitive negotiations with the British and French. He was one of several commissioners named by Congress, but the others were busy elsewhere for the first several months of the discussions. Because of the extreme difficulty of communicating with Congress—it could take two months or more for a letter to cross the Atlantic—Franklin was essentially on his own. When he found that his instructions from Congress did not fit the situation, he ignored them, especially his orders to coordinate all negotiations with the French.

French support for the war was crucial, and Congress wanted to take no chance that the French might withdraw their aid. They instructed Franklin to get French approval for all of his proposals to the British, but Franklin found this completely impractical and unwise—the French had their own interests to safeguard.

Fortunately, the French seemed to understand this as well. Though Franklin often proceeded on his own, the French approved the treaty he worked out.

In the treaty Franklin negotiated, Britain recognized American independence,

A page from the Treaty of Paris bears Benjamin Franklin's signature. The treaty was one of Franklin's greatest accomplishments.

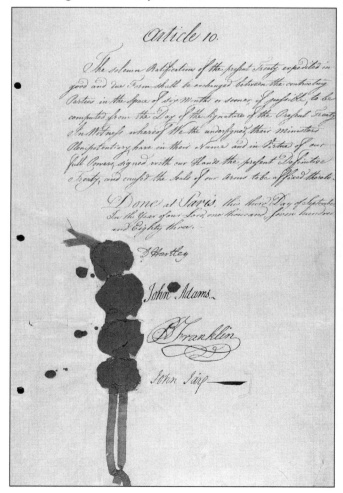

national boundaries and fishing and navigation rights were established, a method of paying old debts was agreed to, and Congress pledged to assist loyalists in regaining their rights and property from the states.

Elder Statesman and Philosopher

After returning to America, Franklin worked on his favorite causes and scientific projects almost until the end of his life, despite painful illnesses. His overriding concern was the welfare of the United States, especially his state, Pennsylvania.

In 1785, Franklin was selected as president of the Supreme Executive Council of Pennsylvania, an office that was much like a modern-day governor. He held the office for three years. He had not intended to accept any position in government—he was nearly eighty years old and in poor health—but the leaders of both of Pennsylvania's political parties asked him to accept the presidency as a way to unify the state after the bitterness of the war years. Franklin was unable to refuse.

Franklin's final service to the United States was as a delegate to the Constitutional Convention in 1787. In his final speech to the convention, read for him by a friend because of Franklin's poor health, he expressed his misgiv-

Balloons

For Franklin, one of the most exciting aspects of being in Paris was the active scientific community there, and the experiments that got the most attention were the first flights of balloons. Franklin witnessed a flight in August 1783 in which a balloon twelve feet in diameter went twenty-four miles. Then in December of that year he saw the second manned flight. (The following account is from *Benjamin Franklin: His Life as He Wrote It.*)

> Between one and two o'clock all eyes were gratified with seeing it [the balloon] rise majestically from among the trees, and ascend gradually above the buildings, a most beautiful spectacle. When it was about two hundred feet high, the brave adventurers held out and waved a little white pennant, on both sides their car, to salute the spectators, who returned loud claps of applause. The wind was very little, so that the object, though moving to the northward, continued long in view; and it was a great while before the admiring people began to disperse. . . . When it arrived at its height, which I suppose might be three or four hundred toises [nineteen hundred to twenty-five hundred feet], it appeared to have only horizontal motion. I had a pocket-glass [telescope] with which I followed it, till I lost sight, first of the men, then of the car, and when I last saw the balloon it appeared no bigger than a walnut.

ings about the Constitution but also his eagerness to be proved wrong:

> I consent, sir, to this Constitution, because I expect no better, and because I am not sure that it is not the best. . . . I hope . . . that we shall act heartily and unanimously in recommending this Constitution, wherever our influence may extend, and turn our future thought and endeavours to the means of having it *well administered.*[11]

Franklin devoted his last years to the abolition of slavery. He proposed that slaves not only be freed but educated so that they could assume productive and responsible roles in society. He had observed a school for the children of freed slaves and judged that the African American children were just as bright and capable of learning as white children. He was disappointed that the new Constitution did not abolish slavery, and he hoped the institution would not last long.

Benjamin Franklin died at his home in Philadelphia on April 17, 1790. In his will he asked for a simple headstone with the inscription. "Benjamin and Deborah Franklin, 1790."[12]

Chapter 2

Paul Revere

Paul Revere was one of the outstanding citizen-patriots of the American Revolution. He was not a great political philosopher or military leader, and he never held high public office, but he was always willing to serve and to risk his life and fortune for the Revolution. According to historians Henry Steele Commager and Richard Morris, Revere "gallops through the Revolution like a centaur,"[13] [a mythical creature who was half man and half horse]. Revere was the most effective alarm and message rider of the early revolutionary period, when communication was vital to the fledgling movement for independence. Messengers had to be intelligent, resourceful, and daring; they also had to be skilled riders. Revere was all these and more.

A sturdy, hardworking man of medium height with a ready smile, Paul Revere was a great joiner, and in his day in Boston there were many political and social groups to join. Revere had a large circle of friends, and everyone in Boston knew who he was and his reputation for honesty and action. To the Whigs—the supporters of American rights and independence—he was a solid and reliable patriot, a man who could get things done. Tories—loyalists who opposed independence from Britain—knew his record for getting the word of troop movements and other news out to the local militias.

Childhood

Paul Revere's father, Apollos Rivoire, was a French Huguenot (Protestant) who was sent by his family first to the Isle of Guernsey and then to Boston to avoid religious persecution by the Catholic king of France. Apollos was only thirteen when he arrived in America, apprenticed to a silversmith. He learned quickly and was good at his trade. When his master died in 1722, Apollos bought his release from his apprenticeship and set up his own shop.

Within a few years he changed his name to Revere because "the bumpkins pronounce it easier,"[14] but still it was not easy for him to make a living. He narrowly avoided bankruptcy, but through hard work and frugal living he was well enough established by 1729 to get married. His wife was Deborah Hitchborn, daughter of a family that owned several businesses on the Boston waterfront. Paul Revere was the third of their thirteen children, born in late December 1734 (the exact day is uncertain).

At the age of 13 Paul Revere became an apprentice in the silversmith trade.

Paul probably attended Boston North Writing School, which was designed to give future tradesmen the basic knowledge of reading, writing, and arithmetic they would need as independent business owners. His formal education probably stopped when he was thirteen years old because that was when most boys signed their indentures, legal contracts binding them to work for a master in their chosen trade. Revere apprenticed as a silversmith and engraver with his father. He also learned to work in gold, copper, and brass because there were several silversmiths in Boston and Paul needed to bring in other sorts of business. He even learned how to make false teeth.

Instigator

Revere was a joiner and organizer from an early age. When he was a teenager he and some of his friends formed a bell-ringers society and wrote to the rector of

Christ Church, which had the largest and best set of bells in Boston, asking permission to ring the bells two hours a week. Their letter reveals a great deal about Revere and the way he would later think about his civic duties during the Revolution:

> We the Subscribers Do agree To the Following Articles Viz [namely] that if we can have the Liberty [permission] From the wardens of Doctor Cuttler's church we will attend there once a week on Evenings to ring the Bells for two hours Each time from the date hereof for one year. . . .

> That None shall be admitted a Member of this Society without Unanimous Vote of the Members then Present and that No Member Shall begg Money of any Person for the Tower [that is, for ringing the bells] on Penalty of being excluded from the Society and that we will attend To Ring any Time when the Wardens of the Church Aforesaid shall desire it on Penalty of Paying three shillings for the good of the Society . . . all differences to be decided by a Majority of Voices.[15]

Historian David Hackett Fischer believes that the bell ringers' letter clearly demonstrates the roots of Revere's passion for the Revolutionary cause:

> This simple document, drawn up by Boston boys barely in their teens,

summarizes many of the founding principles of New England: the sacred covenant and the rule of law, self-government and majority vote, fundamental rights and free association, private responsibility and public duty, the gospel of service and the ethic of work, and a powerful idea of community.[16]

Young Soldier

There is a story that while a boy Paul went to hear Jonathon Mayhew preach at the West Street Church. Mayhew was the most radical and outspoken of the Boston ministers and one of the most important political writers of his day. According to biographer Esther Forbes, "If Paul took to going over to the West Street Church in 1750, there were things being said by Mr. Mayhew which might upset a cautious father and interest a bright, fifteen-year-old boy. . . . In January of that year young Mr. Mayhew fired what John Adams was to call 'the opening gun of the Revolution.'"[17]

That "opening gun" was a sermon that touched off a furious debate on both sides of the Atlantic about the limits of royal and church power. In it Mayhew said that "a spirit of domination is always to be guarded against, both in church and state,"[18] words that fired the growing spirit of independence among young people like Paul Revere.

Though some loyalists were alarmed by talk of independence, Paul Revere certainly did not see himself as a traitor to Britain in those days. In 1755 Revere enlisted in the Massachusetts militia for a British military expedition against the French. Though Revere went on a British expedition, he probably had very little contact with British troops. This fact, and the reasons that colonial troops and British regulars were kept separate would help to form Revere's opinions and actions in later years. According to historian Fred Anderson:

[Massachusetts governor William] Shirley wanted to keep provincials apart from regulars because . . . two British military policies would wreck a campaign in which the two kind of forces had to operate together. First . . . that all provincial officers (that is, all officers commissioned by the governors of colonies) would be deemed junior to all regular officers (those holding commissions issued by the king or his commander in chief). This order reduced the most experienced colonial military leaders, colonels and generals not excepted, to a level below that of the newest pimpled ensign in the regular [British] army.

The second British regulation was that whenever colonial troops operated in conjunction with regulars, they were subject to British military discipline. Anderson continues,

The extension of regular discipline to provincial armies would discourage if

not put a stop to enlistment, for no matter how patriotic or eager for pay potential recruits might be, they knew very well that regular courts-martial routinely sentenced soldiers to severe whippings, and not infrequently to death, for infractions of discipline.[19]

Paul Revere's enlistment was for no more than one year and only for the British expedition against the French in northern New York. Revere was commissioned a second lieutenant, an indication that he stood out from the other recruits. His regiment left Boston in the spring of 1756 and marched across Massachusetts and New York to Fort Oswego on the shore of Lake Ontario. The soldiers suffered from illness, insects, and raiding parties, but Revere escaped injury and returned to Boston with his unit in December.

Within two years, the French were defeated and the threat they posed to Boston was eliminated. This success made British troops very popular in New England in the years following the war. But in the 1760s issues of taxation dramatically erased the good feeling of the colonists.

Business Owner and Leader

Just as Apollos Rivoire became an independent business owner after the death of his teacher, so did Paul. The difference, of course, was that Paul's teacher was also his father. Apollos had died in July 1754, and after Paul's return from military service he settled in as manager of the shop.

Revere became a leader of the skilled laborers in Boston, known as mechanics. In the past, most political power had been in the hands of the wealthy and ed-

Joseph Warren was instrumental in the Boston revolutionary movement.

ucated, but in New England in the mid–eighteenth century, men like Revere were becoming more involved in political affairs. Revere was a leader because of his outspoken views and good judgment, but also because he was a member of overlapping groups of political activists. David Hackett Fischer studied seven prominent groups in Boston in the years leading up to the Revolution and found that twenty-seven men were members of at least two groups, but only two men were members of five: Paul Revere and his friend Dr. Joseph Warren. Between them, they were members of six out of the seven. This meant that Revere and Warren probably knew more than anyone else about the opinions and plans of the Boston revolutionaries, allowing them to play a vital role in transmitting news and coordinating activities.

Warren and Revere were a good team because their backgrounds and talents were so different. Joseph Warren was a popular physician and was exceptionally well connected—he was John Adams's doctor and had worked closely with other Boston revolutionary leaders such as Sam Adams, John Hancock, and James Otis. He was also a talented writer and orator.

Revere was cheerful, gregarious, and popular among his fellow mechanics. His military experience, his reputation for honesty and action, and his obvious good sense meant that he was trusted by the leaders who planned acts of resistance against the British. The friendship of Revere and Warren tied together the two halves of the Revolutionary movement in Boston—the men of property and the mechanics.

Young Revolutionary

In August 1757 Revere married Sarah Orne, with whom he had eight children. Revere tended to be stocky with dark brown hair and a skeptical, penetrating gaze, at least as his likeness was captured by the renowned painter John Singleton Copley around 1770. Sarah died in 1773, and Revere later married Rachel Walker, with whom he also had eight children. Of Paul Revere's sixteen children, five died within a few years of their birth and another five as young adults, most as a result of disease.

Revere's first direct involvement in Revolutionary activities was in 1765. The Boston economy was already in a slump when the British government announced a new set of taxes called the Stamp Act. Revere joined a group of activists known as the Sons of Liberty, and the protests he participated in helped to gain the repeal of the taxes.

Paul Revere holds a piece of silverware in a painting by John Singleton Copley.

Two years later the British Parliament passed the Townshend Acts, which taxed such goods as glass, lead, paper, and tea to raise money to pay for the British army stationed in the colonies. According to Fischer:

The legislature of Massachusetts responded with a Circular Letter to its sister colonies, urging all to resist as one. British leaders were so outraged that the King himself ordered the Massachusetts Circular Letter to be rescinded. The legislature refused by

[January 1770]

WILLIAM JACKSON,

an *IMPORTER*; at the

BRAZEN HEAD,

North Side of the TOWN-HOUSE,

and *Oppofite the Town-Pump, in*

Corn-hill, BOSTON.

It is defired that the Sons and DAUGHTERS of *LIBERTY*, would not buy any one thing of him, for in fo doing they will bring Difgrace upon *themfelves*, and their *Pofterity*, for *ever* and *ever*, AMEN.

A January 1770 notice entreats patriots to boycott all British goods.

"Rescinders' Bowl" became a cherished icon of the American freedom.[20]

Revere's most famous engraving, though, was of the Boston Massacre in March 1770, when British soldiers killed five Bostonians. Based on a drawing by a local artist, it shows the troops firing on an unarmed crowd. Actually, several in the crowd had clubs, at least one soldier had been knocked down, and many were shouting for the soldiers to be killed. None of this became clear, however, until the trial of the soldiers several months later, and Revere's engraving was another potent tool in recruiting young men to the cause of resistance to British rule.

In 1772 the Massachusetts Committee of Correspondence was formed. The establishment of committees of correspondence was a significant step toward the union of the colonies and independence. Patriots in all of the colonies realized that if they acted alone, the British could easily defeat them. But if they could develop a coordinated plan of ac-

a vote of 92 to 17. Paul Revere was commissioned by the Sons of Liberty to make a silver punch bowl commemorating the "Glorious 92." The

tion, they had a chance of success. Revere was one of the principal couriers for the Massachusetts committee.

In 1773 Revere helped organize and participated in the Boston Tea Party, in which Boston patriots dressed as Indians dumped over three hundred chests of tea into Boston Harbor to protest the tea tax. Revere became well known locally, as indicated by the lyrics of a popular ballad:

Paul Revere's most famous engraving illustrates the Boston Massacre in 1770.

Rally Mohawks! Bring out your axes,
And tell King George we'll pay no
    taxes
On his foreign tea . . .

Our [Joseph] Warren's there, and
    bold [Paul] Revere
With hands to do and words to cheer
For Liberty and laws.[21]

In response to tea-tax protests, the British sealed off Boston Harbor and landed troops in June 1774. Revere made an engraving of the landing that clearly expressed his opinion that the British had committed an unjustified act of aggression against the colony. The engraving was printed and widely distributed, help-ing to increase support for protests and Revere's reputation as a patriot.

In December 1774 Revere rode to Portsmouth, New Hampshire, to warn the local militia that the British were sending troops to reinforce Fort William and Mary. Revere convinced the militia commanders to attack, the fort was taken without bloodshed, and its store of gunpowder was hidden in the town.

The Midnight Ride

It was several months before Revere rode on another major mission. It had been

Revere's engraving depicting the British landing at Boston Harbor was widely distributed and helped increase support for protests.

A Grim Duty for a Friend

When Revere's friend Joseph Warren died during the Battle of Bunker Hill, his body was buried in Charlestown by the British troops, who held the town for several months. After they left, Warren's family and friends, including Revere, searched for his grave so that he could be given a proper burial. They were led to a grave that might be that of Warren, but the body was so badly decomposed that even his family members were unsure. According to Esther Forbes, in her book *Paul Revere and the World He Lived In*:

Paul Revere settled the question once and for all. He had fastened in for his friend shortly before Lexington two artificial teeth. Not many of the hundreds buried there on Bunker Hill would have such luxuries. This skull had two. And one was an eye tooth. If further proof was necessary, the silversmith recognized his own silver wire. Perhaps Revere was not the first American dentist to say "Yes, this is he. I recognize my work," but he seems to be the first of whom we have record.

clear to the Boston committees that the British were preparing to send an expedition north to the towns of Lexington and Concord to seize the weapons of the colonial militia and their leaders. Early in April 1775, Revere made two trips there to warn the militia to move its stores of arms to a safe location and to consult on preparations for an attack.

On the night of April 18, 1775, Revere performed his best-known service to the Revolution, what became known as the Midnight Ride. In 1798 he wrote an account of his activities that night in a letter to Dr. Jeremy Belknap:

In the fall of 1774 and winter of 1775, I was one of upwards of thirty, chiefly mechanics, who formed themselves into a committee for the purpose of watching the movements of British soldiers, and gaining every intelligence of the movements of the Tories. We held our meetings at the Green Dragon tavern. We were so careful that our meetings should be kept secret that every time we met, every person swore upon the Bible that they would not discover [talk about] any of our transactions but to Messrs. [John] Hancock, [Sam] Adams, Doctors [Joseph] Warren and [Benjamin] Church and one or two more.[22]

Taverns and inns tended to be identified with one or the other of the loose political confederations, the Whigs and the Tories. This generally helped to keep meetings private and discussions secret, but it failed for Revere's committee because Dr. Church was an informant for General Gage, the royal governor of the Massachusetts Bay Colony. Revere continued,

In the winter, towards the spring, we frequently took turns, two and two, to watch the soldiers by patrolling the streets all night. The Saturday night preceding [Wednesday] the 19th of April, about 12 o'clock at night, the boats belonging to the [British troop] transports were all launched and carried under the sterns of the men-of-war. (They had previously been hauled up and repaired.) We likewise found that the grenadiers and light infantry were all taken off duty.[23]

On Tuesday evening, the patriots' suspicions were further confirmed when the soldiers in Boston began forming up into units. The Whigs assumed that the British regulars were going to march in force to Lexington to arrest Sam Adams and John Hancock, the principal leaders of the Whigs, who were staying there. In fact, the troops were also being sent to Concord to seize a store of arms and ammunition.

The Lights in the Belfry

Revere had been to Lexington the previous weekend to meet with Adams and Hancock, and on his way back he had arranged a way of signaling troop movements with Whigs in Charlestown, across the Charles River from Boston: "I agreed with Colonel Conant and some other gentlemen that if the British went out by water, we would show two lanthorns [lanterns] in the North Church steeple; and if by land, one, as a signal; for we were apprehensive it would be difficult to cross the Charles River or get over Boston Neck."[24] That Tuesday night Revere visited Dr. Warren at his house, where they

Poetry, Not History

Paul Revere's role in the Battle of Lexington and Concord was not widely known before 1861 when Henry Wadsworth Longfellow's poem "Paul Revere's Ride" was first published. It has been read by millions of students ever since. But Longfellow was more concerned with telling a good story than with sticking to the facts, and so people have gotten an inaccurate picture of what Revere did. For example, according to Longfellow,

> He [Revere] said to his friend, "If the British march
> By land or sea from the town to-night,
> Hang a lantern aloft in the belfry arch
> Of the Old North Church tower as a signal light,—
> One, if by land, and two, if by sea;
> And I on the opposite shore will be,
> Ready to ride and spread the alarm
> Through every Middlesex village and farm,
> For the country folk to be up and arm."

In fact, Revere already knew what the Regulars were doing when he left Boston—he asked a friend to signal other patriots in Charlestown in case he did not make it across the river. Longfellow says Revere was the only alarm rider, but both Revere and William Dawes rode that night. The Regulars captured them, however, a fact Longfellow leaves out. Dawes quickly escaped, and though Revere was released before the fighting started, he never reached Concord, his original goal. Nevertheless, Longfellow's poem says, "It was two by the village clock, / When he came to the bridge in Concord town."

discussed the troop movements. Revere then went to the home of his friend Robert Newman, who was sexton (a church officer) of North Church, and told him to signal to the Whigs in Charlestown that the troops were moving by water.

Revere then described what he did that night:

I then went home, took my boots and surtout [overcoat], went to the north part of the town, where I had kept a boat; two friends rowed me across Charles River, a little to the eastward where the *Somerset* man-of-war lay. It was then young flood [low tide], the ship was winding [turning], and the moon was rising. They landed me on the Charlestown side. When I got into town, I met Colonel Conant and several others; they said they had seen our signals. I told them what was acting, and went to get me a horse; I got a horse of Deacon Larkin. While the horse was preparing, Richard Devens, Esq., who was one of the Committee of Safety, came to me and told me that he came down the road from Lexington after sundown that evening; that he met ten British officers, all well mounted, and armed, going up the road.[25]

The horse Revere rode was one of the best saddle mounts in the colony, known as Brown Beauty. Early in his ride that night, Revere came upon two officers of the regulars who tried to arrest him. Brown Beauty outran them, and it was this that allowed Revere to get first to Medford to alert the town's captain of militia and then to Menotomy (now Arlington). He roused houses all along the road to Lexington, where he met with Sam Adams and John Hancock. While they were talking, the other alarm rider, William Dawes, arrived, and together they set out for Concord. Revere continued:

We were overtaken by a young Dr. Prescott, whom we found to be a high Son of Liberty. I told them of the ten officers that Mr. Devens met, and that it was probable we might be stopped before we got to Concord. . . . I likewise mentioned that we had better alarm all the inhabitants till we got to Concord. The young doctor much approved of it and said he would stop with either of us, for the people between that [place] and Concord knew him and would give the more credit to what we said.[26]

Capture

About halfway to Concord, Dawes and Prescott stopped at a house to spread the alarm, and Revere rode ahead a short distance. Revere saw two men on horseback on the road waiting in the same way the two British officers had earlier that night. Revere called for Prescott and Dawes to join him, but as soon as he did four more regulars came out of the shadows and surrounded them. Prescott managed to jump his horse over a stone wall and rode on to Concord, but another six regulars

Paul Revere warns patriots of the arriving British in his now-famous midnight ride.

rode out of the woods, and Revere was soon captured and told to dismount. Dawes managed to escape and headed back toward Lexington. Revere explained that

One of them, who appeared to have the command, examined me, where I came from and what my name was. I told him. He asked me if I was an express [messenger]. I answered in the affirmative. He demanded what time

I left Boston. I told him, and added . . . that there would be five hundred Americans [militia] there in a short time, for I had alarmed the country all the way up. He immediately rode toward those who stopped us, when all five of them came down upon a full gallop. One of them, whom I afterwards found to be Major Mitchel, of the 5th Regiment, clapped his pistol to my head, called me by name and told me he was going to ask me some questions, and if I did not give him true answers, he would blow my brains out.[27]

The First Shots

The British soldiers took Revere toward Lexington. On the way they heard a volley of musket fire. Historians have guessed that this was the militia following the usual practice of firing off loaded weapons before going indoors, in this case, before they went into the tavern. The regulars could tell from the sound that a large number of militia members were close by. They let the prisoners go (after taking their horses) and rode on toward Lexington. Revere walked cross-country back to Concord to tell Adams and Hancock what had happened. First he took them to another house thought to be safer for them, and then Revere walked back to Lexington to get a trunk full of Hancock's confidential militia papers. Just as Revere and another man were hauling the heavy trunk through the lines of the militia to hide it, the regulars arrived. Revere wrote:

> When we had got about one hundred yards from the meeting-house, the British troops appeared on both sides of the meeting-house. In their front was an officer on horseback. They made a short halt; when I saw, and heard, a gun fired, which appeared to be a pistol. Then I could distinguish two guns, and then a continual roar of musketry; when we made off with the trunk.[28]

For the rest of the day, the militias drove the British back to Boston, which the regulars then sealed off. Revere was forced to stay in Cambridge with only the clothes on his back. He was able to get a message to his wife, Rachel, and she tried to send him a letter and money. Unfortunately, she asked Dr. Church, the British

Paul Revere's Row

A question that has puzzled historians for over two centuries is why Paul Revere was not seen and captured while he was being rowed from Boston to Charlestown. In his own account he says that the moon was full and bright that night and that he and his companions rowed within sight of the British ship *Somerset*.

Modern astronomers have answered the question by calculating the precise position of the moon and the time it rose that night. They say that moonrise was at 9:53 that night, perhaps forty-five minutes before Revere's boat trip from Boston. This meant that the moon was still very low in the sky during the trip, and the buildings on the Boston side of the river would have kept Revere's boat in shadow. This was a lucky fact that Revere may not have noticed that night and apparently did not remember years later when he wrote about the experience.

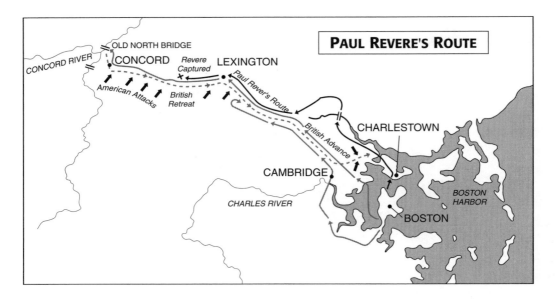

spy, to deliver the envelope to Revere. Church gave it instead to General Gage, in whose papers the letter was found two hundred years later.

The Penobscot Expedition

In June 1775 Paul Revere suffered a great personal loss when his friend Joseph Warren, who had been made a major general of the militia, was killed during the Battle of Bunker Hill. Though saddened, Revere worked diligently for the Massachusetts Committee of Safety in Cambridge, helping to recruit, house, and feed the thousands of militiamen who came to the area to keep the British bottled up in Boston. Revere also printed money for the Continental Congress, designed the first colonial seal, and established a gunpowder mill at Canton, Massachusetts. But soon he became dissatisfied with

these duties and decided to join the army. He was made a major in the Massachusetts militia in April 1776, and he was promoted to lieutenant colonel that November. In 1778 he was named commander of Castle William, a fort on one of the Boston Harbor islands.

Revere wanted a field command, and his chance came when he was named commander of artillery for an expedition to Penobscot Bay in Maine in July 1779. The purpose of the mission was to capture a British outpost then under construction, which when completed would support warships that could harass shipping going to and from Massachusetts ports. Without approval from Congress, Massachusetts mounted an attack that included over two thousand men on nearly forty ships, about half of them warships. They would face a British force of about eight hundred whose fortifications were incomplete.

The expedition was a disaster. Despite overwhelming superiority in numbers, the militia's army commander refused to launch a direct attack. After two weeks of futile artillery barrages by Revere and his men and minor infantry skirmishes, British reinforcements arrived by sea from New York. Instead of fighting through the British line of ships so that they could retreat to Boston, the militia sailed up the Penobscot River. Pursued by the British ships, they were soon forced to run their craft aground and flee into the forest. The Americans lost nearly five hundred men; the British lost thirteen. What was worse, the British completed their fort and maintained an outpost there for the duration of the war.

It was a terrible disappointment for Revere for many reasons: It was a defeat for the cause he loved, men he knew and liked had been killed, and it was probably his last chance for glory in battle. But a further disappointment came soon after. In an effort to find someone to blame, officials court-martialed several of the commanders of the expedition, including Revere. Revere knew that he had done nothing wrong and was eager to clear his name, but it was over two years

before his case was heard. In the end, he was acquitted.

Civic Leader

Because of the Penobscot disaster, Revere was relieved of his command of Castle William. But it did not take him long to find other ways to be useful. He participated in a wide variety of activities in support of the war, and he went back to his trade. He became a well-known goldsmith and silversmith, and his foundry cast many of the fittings for the naval vessel USS *Constitution*, known now as *Old Ironsides*.

Even at age sixty-five he was willing to take a risk: He established the first copper-rolling mill in North America, which supplied sheet copper for the domes of such buildings as the Massachusetts State House and New York City Hall. It also rolled the copper to refit the *Constitution* in 1803 before it sailed for North Africa and duty in the Barbary Wars.

Revere worked hard for ratification of the federal Constitution and was always interested in politics, both national and local. His later years were clouded by the deaths of his wife and eldest son, but Paul Revere remained active and relatively healthy until his final illness. He died on May 10, 1818.

Chapter 3

John Adams

John Adams had one of the longest and most distinguished careers of public service in the history of America, and he played a vital role in the Revolution as a thinker, a catalyst for the movement, and a diplomat. After the Revolutionary War he continued as a diplomat, serving in France and Great Britain. In 1788 he returned to America, and in 1789 he became the nation's first vice president, serving under George Washington. Adams was elected president in 1796. He retired to his Massachusetts farm in 1801 but continued to comment on politics and to influence his son, John Quincy Adams, who was elected president in 1824.

Childhood

John Adams was born on October 31, 1735, in Braintree (now Quincy), Massachusetts, about ten miles south of Boston. The Adams family had been in Braintree since 1638. They were farmers who in the winter worked at other trades. They were a big family—Henry, the first Adams in Massachusetts, had eighty-nine grandchildren. Adams's father, also named John, was a deacon in his church, a farmer, and a maltster (one who malted barley for use in bread and beer). Adams's mother Susanna was a member of the prominent and wealthy Boylston family. Religion was central to Adams's family. In a letter to his friend Benjamin Rush, Adams wrote, "What has preserved this race of Adamses in all their ramifications in such Numbers, health, peace, Comfort, and Mediocrity? I believe it is Religion, without which they would have been Rakes, Fops, Sots, Gamblers, starved with hunger, or frozen with cold . . . melted away and disappeared."[29]

Adams's mother was probably illiterate, but his father was widely read and both parents valued education. Adams went to school in the Braintree area until he was fifteen, when he applied to and was accepted by Harvard College, located just north of Boston in Cambridge. He got a partial scholarship and spent four years at Harvard, which he described as among the happiest of his life. Though a good student before he went to college, at Harvard he developed what was to be a lifelong love of books. He graduated in 1755, third in his class academically.

His years at Harvard were Adams's first time away from home and parental control, and Adams showed that though still quite young, he knew how to balance his freedom and responsibilities. In four years his only infraction of the rules was extending a stay at home in Braintree longer than he had permission for.

Adams studied hard, but he also found time to make firm friendships, many of which lasted the rest of his life. According to biographer David McCullough, Adams "had a talent for friendship. To many he seemed prickly, intractable, and often he was, but as his friend Jonathan Sewall would write, Adams had 'a heart formed for friendship, and susceptible to the finest feelings.' He needed friends, prized old friendships."[30]

Teacher and Student

Mrs. Adams wanted her son to be a minister, but she was perhaps the only one who thought he was actually suited for the profession. With the encouragement of friends at Harvard and the permission of his father, Adams decided to become a lawyer. First, though, he had to earn enough money to pay his apprenticeship fee. He did this by finding a job as a teacher in Worcester, Massachusetts, fifty miles to the west.

After a year he had enough money to begin his apprenticeship with a lawyer, James Putnam of Worcester. Adams studied law at night and continued teaching during the day for the next two years. He passed his bar exam in Boston and began his practice in November 1759. The few lawyers in the colony had to travel with the court to argue their cases, going as far north as Maine, which was then part of

John Adams was America's first vice president.

the Massachusetts Bay Colony. Adams was frequently away from home.

Adams graduated from Harvard, where he developed a life-long love of books.

Courtship and Marriage

When he was twenty-four John Adams met his future wife, Abigail Smith. She was a small, frail child of fifteen who probably looked even younger, and he was not attracted to her. They were reintroduced two years later because one of Adams's friends was courting Abigail's sister. In the interim Abigail had become a lovely, vivacious young woman, and they soon fell in love.

Abigail was the daughter of William Smith, a minister, and her mother was a member of the Quincy family, one of the wealthiest in the area. Mrs. Smith did not approve of John Adams, the son of a farmer, courting her daughter, but the young couple persisted and eventually won her over.

John's law practice kept him on the road a good part of the year, but fortunately Abigail and John were both excellent and prolific letter writers. One of John's earliest letters to his future wife, written in August 1763, shows the humor

The educated and shrewd Abigail Adams often served as a worthy political adviser to her husband, John.

and affection that would always characterize their correspondence, especially during their later separations while Adams was away tending to his political duties:

I lay, in the well known Chamber, and dreamed, I saw a Lady, tripping it over the Hills, on Weymouth shore, and Spreading Light and Beauty and Glory, all around her. At first I thought it was Aurora [dawn], with her fair Complexion, her Crimson Blushes and her million Charms and Graces. But I soon found it was Diana [Abigail], a Lady infinitely dearer to me and more charming.[31]

Adams's relationship with Abigail was unusually close and confiding. At a time when women had few opportunities for education, Abigail had been given excellent tutors and loved reading. She was also politically astute and a good judge of character, a steadying influence on Adams, who was subject to volcanic bursts of anger. John's devotion to and dependence on Abigail continued throughout their life together. She was an important adviser to him during the Revolutionary War, but even more so during his terms as vice president and president.

Lawyer and Family Man

Adams's legal practice flourished, and he became respected for his skill and honesty. He was made a member of the Braintree town council, he was responsible for highway surveying in the area, and he was attorney for the city of Boston in the looming crisis over British attempts to tax the colony.

Along with his legal practice, Adams's family was also growing. A daughter, Abigail (known as Nabby) was born in 1765. She was followed by three sons: John Quincy in 1767, Charles in 1770, and Thomas Boylston in 1772. A second daughter, Elizabeth, was stillborn in 1777.

Adams loved his farm and family and a predictable life full of routine and time to work outdoors, to walk, to ride horseback, and to study. But the demands of his work kept him away from home. In May 1772 he wrote to Abigail, "I wish myself at Braintree. . . . I want to see my wife and Children every Day, I want to see my Grass and Blossoms and Corn, &c. every Day. I want to see my Workmen, nay I almost want to go and see the Bosse Calfs's [cows]. . . . But above all except the Wife and Children I want to see my Books."[32]

The Stamp Act Crisis

John Adams began his career as a patriot in 1765 during the Stamp Act crisis, a British attempt to tax the colonies that sparked numerous protests. Adams wrote his views on the situation in an essay called "A Dissertation on the Common and the Feudal Laws." The essay expressed Adams's belief that the rights the colonists were demanding were not new ideas of their own invention but rather rights already guaranteed to them under British law. Furthermore, he thought these rights should be enjoyed by Americans because they and their ancestors had risked their lives to cross the ocean and establish the colonies. Adams wrote,

> Let it be known that British liberties are not the grants of princes or parliaments . . . that many of our rights are inherent and essential, agreed on as maxims and established as preliminaries, even before Parliament existed. . . . Let us read and recollect and impress upon our souls the views and ends of our more immediate forefathers, in exchanging their native country [England] for a dreary, inhospitable wilderness. . . . Recollect their amazing fortitude, their bitter sufferings—the hunger, the nakedness, the cold, which they patiently endured. . . . Recollect the civil and religious principles and hopes and expectations which constantly supported and carried them through all hardships with patience and resignation. Let us recollect it was liberty, the hope of liberty, for them selves and us and ours, which conquered all discouragements, dangers, and trials.[33]

An angry mob demands that a stamp agent resign his job, part of the protests over the Stamp Act of 1765.

Later in 1765 Adams drafted the instructions for Braintree's representative in the colonial legislature, in which he clearly stated the colonists' argument against taxation without representation. The Stamp Act was repealed in 1766, and for a few years tensions between the colonies and Britain eased. But an issue was brewing that threatened to erupt in violence—the presence of British troops in Boston.

The Boston Massacre

John Adams was in Boston having dinner with friends on the evening of March 5, 1770. About nine o'clock they heard the bells normally used as a fire alarm, and they went outside to investigate. Years later, Adams wrote in his *Autobiography*, "In the Street We were informed that the British Soldiers had fired on the Inhabitants, killed some and wounded others near the Town house. A Croud of People was flowing down the Street, to the Scene of the Action."[34]

British troops and colonists fight in the event that became known as the Boston Massacre.

Adams went home quickly, partly because it seemed that the disturbance was over and partly because Abigail was pregnant and he was afraid the alarm bells would upset her. The next morning he was asked to defend the soldiers who had fired on the crowd and their commanding officer, Captain Preston—they had all been arrested and charged with murder. The other Boston lawyers would not take the case because they were afraid of the anger of the people of Boston. Adams later wrote, "I had no hesitation in answering that Council [a lawyer] ought to be the very last thing that an accused Person should want in a free Country."[35]

Adams managed to get the trials delayed several months, allowing tempers to cool. In defending the men, Adams argued that though the soldiers had fired on the crowd, they were innocent of murder—instead, the British government was guilty for having put the troops in Boston in the first place. In his summation at the trial of the soldiers he said, "Soldiers quartered in a populous town will always occasion two mobs where they prevent one. They are wretched conservators of the peace."[36] Adams wanted the jurors to put themselves in the position of the soldiers, painting a vivid picture of the scene the night of the shooting. He told them,

[T]he soldiers had no friends about them; with all the bells ringing, to call the town together to assist the people in King-street . . . the people shouting, huzzaing, and making the mob whistle . . . the people crying Kill them! Kill them! Knock them over! heaving snow-balls, oyster shells, clubs, white birch sticks three inches and a half diameter, consider yourselves, in this situation, and then judge, whether a reasonable man in the soldiers situation, would not have concluded they were going to kill him.[37]

Adams's arguments convinced the juries. All the soldiers were acquitted of murder, though two were found guilty of manslaughter, for which they were branded on their thumbs. Some Bostonians respected Adams for his courage in defending the soldiers, but others were angry with him. Adams knew that avoiding politics would be good for his legal

practice, but he could not betray his principles. And when the next major public protest occurred, the Boston Tea Party of December 1773, Adams loudly and publicly approved of it.

Delegate to the Continental Congress

Adams was one of five Massachusetts delegates to the First Continental Congress in Philadelphia, which met during September and October 1774. He was quickly recognized as one of the most astute thinkers in the Congress. He assisted in writing a declaration of grievances to the king and a summary of the rights of British subjects in America. He worked from dawn until well after dark every day except Sunday, when he went to two or even three church services. Congress adjourned with an agreement to reconvene in May of the next year if their demands had not been met.

Nothing came from the petitions of the first Congress, and so the Second Continental Congress convened in Philadelphia on May 10, 1775, less than a month after the Battle of Lexington and Concord. Though not a participant in the battle, Adams knew many men who were and saw its effects firsthand: wounded patriot militia men, grieving families, and a blockaded Boston where the necessities of life were becoming scarce. Conditions only worsened following the Battle of Bunker Hill and the burning of Charlestown by the British on June 17, 1775. It was hard

The First Continental Congress meets in Carpenter's Hall, Philadelphia. John Adams attended as one of five delegates from Massachusetts.

for Adams to be away from Abigail and the children that summer, but he knew that the debate in this session of Congress would decide the fate of the colonies.

Adams was assigned to several important committees, and he was nearly overwhelmed with the enormity of the tasks that he and his fellow delegates had taken on. He wrote to Abigail,

When 50 or 60 Men have a Constitution to form for a great Empire, at the same Time that they have a Country of fifteen hundred Miles extent to fortify, Millions to arm and train, a Naval

Power to begin, an extensive Commerce to regulate, numerous Tribes of Indians to negotiate with, a standing Army of Twenty seven Thousand Men to raise, pay, victual [feed] and officer, I really shall pity those 50 or 60 men.[38]

The major conflict in the Congress was between those who wanted to prepare for war and those who wanted to try again to negotiate with British authorities. The latter camp was led by John Dickinson, a wealthy and highly respected Philadelphia lawyer, while Adams was among the most outspoken advocates for military preparation, believing that this alone would bring Britain to the bargaining table.

Dickinson proposed sending one final letter to King George asking for an end to military action and talks on the colonies' grievances. The letter came to be known as the Olive Branch Petition, and the debate over it was especially heated, leading to a loud argument between Dickinson and Adams that continued outside the meeting hall. Adams later wrote a letter critical of Dickinson that was intercepted and published. This made Adams very unpopular for a time both with his fellow delegates and with the townspeople of Philadelphia.

The Olive Branch Petition was approved and taken to England, but King George refused even to see the American ambassador. Congress learned of the total failure of this effort at peace in November 1775. This convinced most members of Congress that Adams had been right all along.

Adams did not want to go to war with Britain, but he saw that there was no longer any way to patch up the relationship. On May 15, 1776, he wrote the preamble to a resolution calling on the colonies to ignore the dictates of the British colonial

King George refused all peace efforts made by the American patriots.

authorities and begin forming their own independent governments. Adams knew that this was one of the pivotal days in the history of America. He wrote to Abigail, "G[reat] B[ritain] has at last driven America, to the last Step, a compleat Seperation from her, a total absolute Independence, not only of her Parliament but of her Crown [king], for such is the Amount [effect] of the resolve of the 15th [of May 1776]."[39]

The Declaration of Independence

Congress adjourned so that the delegates could go back to the colonies to talk over the decision for independence. In the meantime, Congress picked Adams to be on the committee to draft a declaration of independence. The committee included Benjamin Franklin and Thomas Jefferson. Franklin was highly respected but not a lawyer. Jefferson was a lawyer but eight years younger than Adams and not as well known to the delegates—he seldom spoke during debates or even in committee meetings. According to biographer John Ferling, "At the initial meeting of the panel, Adams was offered the assignment of drafting the declaration. He declined. No one, least of all Adams, imagined the immortality that such an act would bring. . . .The committee next turned to Jefferson."[40]

When Congress reconvened, it first debated whether to declare independence. This decision was voted on and passed on July 2. Then the question of

"A Most Sensible and Forcible Speaker"

Twenty-five years after the Continental Congress convened in Philadelphia, one of the delegates, Dr. Benjamin Rush, wrote his impressions of his fellow members. In the intervening years Rush and Adams had been close friends, and this shows in Rush's description of him, found in *The Spirit of Seventy-Six: The Story of the American Revolution As Told by Participants.*

> He had been educated a lawyer, and stood high in his profession in his native state. He was a most sensible and forcible speaker. Every member of Congress in 1776 acknowledged him to be the first man in the House. Dr. Brownson (of Georgia) used to say when [Adams] spoke, he fancied an angel was let down from heaven to illumine the Congress. He saw the whole of a subject at a single glance, and by a happy union of the powers of reasoning and persuasion often succeeded in carrying measures which were at first sight of an unpopular nature. . . .
>
> He was a stranger to dissimulation [lying], and appeared to be more jealous of his reputation for integrity than for talents or knowledge. He was strictly moral, and at all times respectful to Religion. In speaking of the probable issue of the war he said to me . . . "We shall succeed in our struggle, provided we repent of our sins, and forsake them," and then added, "I will see it out, or go to heaven in its ruins."

the wording had to be settled, so Jefferson's draft was debated, with Adams leading the fight for its adoption. After some revision, it was accepted on July 4.

Adams wrote to Abigail, telling her that "Yesterday the greatest Question was decided, which ever was debated in America, and a greater, perhaps, never was or will be decided among Men."[41] Adams saw the impending war as a time of purification, telling her that "The Furnace of Affliction produces Refinement, in States as well as Individuals."[42]

Adams correctly predicted the importance that future generations would attach to the decision Congress had reached. But on July 3, 1776, he thought that the day of the vote for independence rather than the day the wording of the declaration was approved would be celebrated. He wrote to Abigail:

The Second Day of July 1776 . . . will be celebrated, by succeeding Generations, as the great anniversary Festival. It ought to be commemorated, as the Day of Deliverance by solemn Acts of Devotion to God Almighty. It ought to be solemnized with Pomp and Parade, with Shews, Games, Sports, Guns, Bells, Bonfires and Illuminations [fireworks] from one End of the Continent to the other from this Time forward forever more.[43]

Commissioner to France

In November 1777 Adams was elected commissioner to France. Sailing three thousand miles across the Atlantic was dangerous at any time but especially so in winter and when at war, and taking the post meant a great sacrifice in being away from Abigail and the children, his farm, and his law practice. But John and Abigail decided that their ten-year-old son John Quincy should go with him. They regarded it as part of his education, a chance to see the world. John and John Quincy sailed in February 1778 and arrived in Paris in April.

Benjamin Franklin was already in Paris and was a celebrity as well as a diplomat. Adams respected Franklin's many accomplishments and knew the value of his popularity with both the French nobility and the French people. On the other hand, Adams found some of Franklin's personal habits hard to cope with. In his *Autobiography* he wrote that he and Arthur Lee, another commissioner, "could rarely obtain the Company of Dr. Franklin for a few minutes, and often when I had drawn the Papers . . . for Signature . . . I was frequently obliged to wait several days, before I could procure the Signature of Dr. Franklin to them."[44]

More than Franklin's unavailability perplexed Adams. Arthur Lee and Franklin had become bitter enemies, and their constant arguments made working together nearly impossible. Adams tried to busy himself by reading as much as he could about the political situation in Europe and writing frequent reports to Congress, but after a few months he realized that a different arrangement had to be made—Adams proposed to Congress that

The Drafting Committee

In 1822, John Adams wrote his recollection of the way in which Jefferson was chosen to draft the Declaration of Independence, as quoted in *John Adams: A Biography in His Own Words,* edited by James Bishop Peabody.

The committee [of five] met, discussed the subject, and then appointed Mr. Jefferson and me to make the draught, I suppose because we were the two first on the list. . . .

Jefferson proposed to me to make the draught. I said, "I will not."
"You should do it."
"Oh! no." [Adams said.]
"Why will you not? You ought to do it."
"I will not."
"Why?" [Jefferson asked.]
"Reasons enough."
"What can be your reasons?"
"Reason first—You are a Virginian, and a Virginian ought to appear at the head of this business. Reason second—I am obnoxious, suspected, and unpopular. You are very much otherwise. Reason third—You can write ten times better than I can."
"Well," said Jefferson, "if you are decided, I will do as well as I can."

there be a single commissioner to France. This idea was eventually accepted, though Adams was given no credit for the idea and was not even given a new assignment. This offended him, but he soon decided to return to Boston with John Quincy. They sailed in March 1779, but their ship was detained in port. They finally reached Boston on August 2.

Constitution of the Commonwealth of Massachusetts

Though he felt slighted by Congress, Adams was immediately honored in Massachusetts by being appointed to the committee that would draft the state's constitution. In less than a month in the fall of 1779, Adams drafted the Massachusetts constitution. Adopted in 1780, it is the world's oldest constitution still in effect.

Adams's draft said that governments exist for the benefit of the governed, to safeguard their natural rights. It declared that all citizens are born free and independent with rights to free speech, press, and elections, trial by jury, and protection from unreasonable search and seizure. One of the most remarkable features of the constitution, however, is its emphasis on education. It states that the legislature and other public officials must promote education and the advancement of literature and science, not only for commercial reasons but also to "inculcate the principles of humanity and general benevolence, public and private charity, industry and frugality, honesty and punctuality in their dealings; sincerity, good humor, and all social affections, and generous sentiments among the people."[45]

The Peace of Paris

Adams was not able to stay at home very long. At the end of September 1779 Congress named him peace commissioner to negotiate with the British. He was given sole responsibility for arriving at a treaty for peace and commerce with Great Britain, though no one had any idea what form the talks would take or what obstacles would arise. In fact, a final treaty would not be signed for another four years.

Adams, his ten-year-old son Charles, and John Quincy sailed for Europe in November and reached Paris, where the talks were to take place, in February 1780. The French, who were acting as intermediaries with the British and had their own interests to safeguard, persuaded Adams to keep his role as peace commissioner secret, though it was obvious that the British already knew why he was there. Benjamin Franklin, still the American ambassador to France, did nothing to dissuade the French. As McCullough explains, Vergennes, the French foreign minister,

> found Adams's manifest integrity unsettling; Adams's emphatic patriotism appealed not at all. . . . Preferring to deal only with the ever obliging Franklin, he dreaded the prospect of Adams meddling in what he, Vergennes, regarded as his exclusive domain, the power politics of Europe. . . . Adams . . . was a novice; and there was no telling the damage such a man might do.[46]

Early in the summer of 1780, Vergennes drew Adams into a dispute over the devaluation of U.S. currency, hoping

that Adams would provide evidence of his lack of diplomatic skill. Adams did just that. He wrote several letters defending U.S. policy and criticizing the level of French aid. Vergennes turned the letters over to Franklin, who sent them on to Congress. It would be a year before Adams learned of the effect his letters had had on Congress.

In July 1780 Adams decided that because he was making no progress in France he would go to Holland to try to get recognition of the United States and a loan. Adams's attempts at diplomacy in Holland were complicated, however, by military defeats in America and the defection of Benedict Arnold. The Dutch thought the fledgling nation unlikely to survive and thus a bad credit and diplomatic risk.

Adams was caught in a diplomatic snare. Though everyone knew why he was in Holland, he could not formally present his requests until invited to do so by the Dutch authorities. They were reluctant because this would amount to recognizing the validity of the United States, which Britain, an important trading partner of the Dutch, did not want them to do.

Adams took a bold step. He wrote a long letter to the Dutch authorities explaining his mission and giving a list of reasons Holland should help the United States in its war for independence. He delivered his letter to the Dutch, but knowing that the Dutch might take a long time to reply, he also had it published. It was soon common knowledge in Europe, putting pressure on the Dutch to recognize his mission.

In June 1781 Vergennes asked Adams to return to Paris to discuss a proposal by Russia and Austria to mediate the war. Adams feared that mediation would result in Britain retaining some of the colonies, and so he opposed it. Then he received more bad news, letters demoting him from sole peace commissioner to membership on a commission of five. Ferling writes that "For a man of Adams's vanity, for a man who had sacrificed so much to return to Europe in the belief that he was to play a huge role in securing American independence—a role second only to that of General Washington—this news had to be . . . a staggering refutation of all that he had done and sought to do."[47]

Within two weeks Adams returned to Amsterdam to continue negotiating with the Dutch. He fell ill in August, however, probably from malaria. He was unable to work at all until October and did not feel significantly better until early 1782.

But the fall would also bring good news. In October, the British commander Cornwallis surrendered his army at Yorktown, Virginia. As soon as the news reached Europe, Holland was much more interested in negotiating recognition and trade relations with the United States. For the next several months Adams presided over the development of two treaties with Holland and the establishment of the U.S. embassy there.

In September 1782 the British representative to the peace talks finally received permission to proceed. Franklin took the lead for the Americans in the negotiations, but Adams made many important contributions to the process. The treaty took another ten months to complete. The Treaty of Paris was signed on September 3, 1783, but its signing again left Adams unsure what his next assignment would be.

Ambassador

Adams's role in American independence had been substantial, and he was widely respected. The relationship of the United States with France was vital. Congress wanted experienced representatives there, so it asked Adams and Jefferson to stay on in Paris.

In the summer of 1784, Abigail sailed to France, and she brought their nineteen-year-old daughter Nabby with her. The Adamses developed a close personal relationship with Jefferson while in Paris. He and Adams collaborated on many diplomatic projects, and Jefferson became almost like a second father to John Quincy. Then Adams was appointed envoy to Britain in February 1785. He and Abigail went to London in May, where they stayed for the next three years. His time in London was much more relaxed than the war years had been, but he and Abigail were not entirely happy in England. Adams asked Congress for recall, which was granted in February 1788.

George Washington (center) and John Adams (right) are inaugurated as the first president and vice president of the United States in 1789.

When Adams reached Boston in June, he was greeted like a hero, and it was clear that he could have virtually any job in government that he wanted.

Vice President and President

The only job not open to Adams was that of president. No one doubted that George Washington would be chosen to lead the nation. Adams was elected vice president. He was loyal to Washington during the eight years of his administration, both because Adams respected Washington personally and because their views were very similar. But that did not mean that Washington used Adams as a close adviser. In fact, during his presidency Washington consulted Adams on only two foreign policy issues.

Adams felt neglected and useless. He did not like the job of vice president, calling it "the most insignificant office that ever the invention of man contrived or his imagination conceived."[48] But Adams's patience was finally rewarded when he was elected president in 1796.

Thomas Jefferson was elected vice president. Though during Washington's presidency he and Adams had disagreed on many matters of policy, they still admired each other. They attempted to cooperate together as president and vice president but quickly failed. Throughout most of Adams's presidency, Jefferson actively worked against him, though behind the scenes.

The 1800 contest for the presidency between Adams and Jefferson was one of the most heated campaigns in American history. Jefferson won, but his relationship with Adams was shattered. Adams did not even attend Jefferson's inauguration. It was a loss that both men deeply felt.

Retirement

Adams and Jefferson had no contact for the next eleven years. After much effort, however, their mutual friend Dr. Benjamin Rush cajoled the two into writing. The first letter came from Adams, written on January 1, 1812. He gave Jefferson some family news and closed, "I wish you Sir many happy New Years and that you may enter the next and many succeeding Years with as animating Prospects for the Public as those at present before Us. I am Sir with

long and sincere Esteem your Friend and Servant."[49] Jefferson responded, and thus began one of the most remarkable correspondences in American history.

Abigail, his partner in so many areas of life for nearly six decades, died in October 1818. But Adams lived to see his son John Quincy elected president in 1824. Adams was in failing health but alert and inquisitive until his final illness. It seemed that he wanted to hang on until the fiftieth anniversary of the Declaration of Independence, and he did so, dying on the afternoon of July 4, 1826. Jefferson, his friend and collaborator, had died earlier that day at his home in Virginia. Adams's last words were, "Thomas Jefferson survives."[50]

Chapter 4

Thomas Jefferson

homas Jefferson contributed many of the key ideas that rallied the people of the American colonies to the cause of the Revolution. Some historians have called him the greatest genius of the Revolutionary era, a master of law, diplomacy, and politics who guided his state and the nation for decades as a legislator, governor of Virginia, ambassador, secretary of state, vice president, and president. Jefferson was also an architect, horticulturist, scientist, inventor, and musician. At a 1962 dinner for Nobel Prize winners, President John F. Kennedy remarked, "I think this is the most extraordinary collection of talent, of human knowledge, that has ever been gathered together at the White House, with the possible exception of when Thomas Jefferson dined alone."[51]

Jefferson was on the public stage most of his adult life, achieving fame and admiration throughout America and Europe. Despite this, both people who knew him

and historians have called him enigmatic. They especially puzzle over the fact that he was a slave owner but wrote, "We hold these Truths to be self-evident, that all men are created equal, that they are endowed by their Creator with certain unalienable Rights, that among these are Life, Liberty, and the Pursuit of Happiness."[52]

Jefferson was intensely private—there were areas of his life that he refused to expose. Biographer Fawn Brodie writes that Jefferson wanted to preserve a complete record of his public life but also wanted to keep his private life private:

> Jefferson had a superb sense of history and an exact understanding of his own role in it. He preserved a legacy of over 25,000 letters from his friends and acquaintances, as well as copies of his own letters . . . that numbered 18,000. . . . Still, he destroyed what would have been among the most revealing letters of his life, his

correspondence with his mother and with his wife. He never finished his autobiography, and halfway through this mere fragment of his life numbering only 120 pages, he complained, "I am already tired of talking about myself."[53]

Though a reluctant speaker, Jefferson was a persuasive writer. He argued convincingly that Britain's actions were contrary to its own constitution and statutes, and that they were contrary to natural law. He saw more clearly than most that the colonies must break with Britain and form a new nation, and he conveyed this idea in words that swept many Americans into the movement for independence.

Early Life

Thomas Jefferson was born in rural Virginia on April 13, 1743. His mother was Jane Randolph, a member of one of the richest and most important families in Virginia. His father was Peter Jefferson, a surveyor, planter, and land speculator whose family had been in Virginia for about seventy-five years at the time of

Thomas Jefferson, author of the Declaration of Independence, was a master of law, diplomacy, and politics.

Jefferson's birth. The Jefferson family lived on a plantation called Shadwell on the western edge of British settlement.

Peter Jefferson's holdings were not large by the standards of the Virginia aristocracy, but he was shrewd and tireless, always looking for ways to increase the size of his estate.

Jefferson attended school in this humble-looking schoolhouse.

Peter Jefferson wanted his son Thomas to get the best education possible, partly because he had not had that opportunity himself. At age five Thomas began his education with a teacher of English and basic arithmetic. Then at age nine he went to what was known as a Latin school. He later wrote that "My teacher Mr. Douglas a clergyman from Scotland was but a superficial Latinist, less instructed in Greek, but with the rudiments of these languages he taught me French."[54]

He did well in all his studies, but his greatest talent early in life was for music. He took violin and cello lessons, and his sisters studied the harp and harpsichord. They all sang, and often performed for family gatherings. Jefferson was especially diligent, often practicing three hours a day.

Jefferson's father died in 1757 when Thomas was fourteen. The next year Thomas began attending the school of the Rev. James Maury, located twelve miles from Shadwell. He boarded with the Maurys, becoming like a member of their family, and only went home on weekends.

The College of William and Mary

In 1760 Jefferson began a two-year stay at the only college in Virginia, the College of William and Mary. It was a small school, with seven faculty and about one hundred students. Jefferson became the student—and the lifelong friend—of William Small, the newest member of the college faculty. In his autobiography, Jefferson wrote:

It was my great good fortune, and what probably fixed the destinies of my life that Dr. Wm. Small of Scotland was then professor of Mathematics, a man profound in most of the useful

Thomas Jefferson attended the College of William and Mary in Virginia, pictured here circa 1950.

branches of science, with a happy talent of communication, correct and gentlemanly manners, & an enlarged & liberal mind. He, most happily for me, became soon attached to me & made me his daily companion when not engaged in the school.[55]

At William and Mary, Jefferson was out on his own for the first time, free from what he saw as the restrictions and trivialities of life in his mother's house. He had a supportive and even devoted mentor in Dr. Small, and he had the opportunity to discuss great ideas with learned men. He set himself a rigorous study schedule, much more difficult than was required by the college, and his dedication to learning was rewarded. Soon Dr. Small introduced Jefferson to the governor of Virginia and to George Wythe, the most accomplished attorney in Virginia, who would become Jefferson's mentor in the law, his partner in revolutionary politics, and another lifelong friend.

At times Jefferson studied up to fifteen hours a day, especially while he was at Shadwell. Biographer Willard Sterne Randall believes this was partly due to his realization that he would soon have to assume adult responsibilities: "Jefferson knew that his thirst for knowledge, underwritten by a generous inheritance and inspired by a fortuitous group of teachers, could only be indulged for a limited time."[56]

In addition to Small and Wythe, Jefferson also made many friends among people his own age. As Brodie remarks, "It was rare for a man to know Thomas Jefferson and not cherish the friendship all his life. This was as true of his early youth as during his manhood."[57]

Legal Career

By the time Jefferson graduated from William and Mary, he had lost some of his adolescent awkwardness and had become a striking young man. He was a bit over six feet, two inches tall with fair, freckled skin, red hair, and a slim, muscular build. He was not an enthusiastic hunter and frontiersman like his father had been, but he was one of the best horsemen in all of colonial America.

Jefferson's legal training took five years of study and apprenticeship. According to Brodie, "Jefferson's years under Wythe, years of virtually uninterrupted reading, not only in the law but also in ancient classics, English literature, and general political philosophy, were not so much an apprenticeship for law as an apprenticeship for greatness."[58] Many years later Jefferson himself would say that it was "a time of life when I was bold in the pursuit of knowledge, never fearing to follow truth and reason to whatever results they led and bearding [confronting] every authority which stood in their way."[59]

Jefferson was admitted to the Virginia bar in 1767. He found that he liked the practice of law more than he had expected to. During his training he had thought that he would prefer being a philosopher

Jefferson's Law Curriculum

For two hundred years, Thomas Jefferson has been used to convince struggling law students that their burdens could be much worse. As a lawyer, Jefferson was expected to allow apprentices to study law under his guidance. Jefferson did not do this when he was young because his practice took him around the colony so much that he could not provide adequate supervision. So when prospective students applied to him, he explained his situation and sent them a curriculum to study. One of these survives; it was written around 1770 to a friend named Bernard Moore. (It can be found in Jefferson's *Writings*.) Jefferson told Moore that Greek and Latin were essential, and in addition to the basic law texts of the day, the curriculum included mathematics, astronomy, geography, biology, physics, agriculture, ancient and modern history, ethics, religion, philosophy, literature, rhetoric, and public speaking. At the end of this extensive list of books, Jefferson closed by saying,

These by no means constitute the whole of what might be usefully read in each of these branches of science. The mass of excellent works going into more detail is great indeed. But those here noted will enable the student to select for himself such others of detail as may suit his particular views & dispositions. They will give him a respectable, an useful & satisfactory degree of knowledge in these branches, and will themselves form a valuable and sufficient library for a lawyer, who is at the same time a lover of science.

of law, but the daily round of meeting with clients, researching their cases, and going to court suited him well, at least for a few years. The competent way he handled his busy practice—Jefferson had up to five hundred cases on his books at one time—brought him the respect of his fellow colonists. He was selected to be a justice of the peace, and in 1769, at age twenty-six, he was elected as the delegate to the Virginia House of Burgesses for Albemarle County.

Most of Jefferson's legal practice concerned land law, and he became known as the most expert land lawyer in the colony. Jefferson relied on his learning, meticulous research, and skill in argument to advance the interests of his clients. He also followed in his father's footsteps by dealing in land himself. He was involved in land speculation schemes with friends that skated on the edge of the law. Later, the sort of schemes he had pursued were in fact made illegal.

Political Stirrings

By 1765, when Jefferson was twenty-two, sentiment for revolution was building in Virginia. Jefferson was perfectly situated to participate in the movement. For example, he was present for the first speech as a legislator of one of the firebrands of the Revolution, the twenty-nine-year-old Patrick Henry. Jefferson later wrote, "I attended the debate . . . of the H[ouse] of Burgesses, & heard the splendid display of Mr. Henry's talents as a popular orator. They were great indeed; such as I have never heard from any other man."[60]

Jefferson was one of those who saw that the colonies' opposition to Britain could be effective only if they found a way to work together. He supported forming a committee of correspondence for Virginia. Other colonies were establishing similar committees so that news of political decisions and other developments could be transmitted up and down the East Coast more efficiently. In his *Autobi-* *ography* he wrote, "We were all sensible that the most urgent of all measures was that of coming to an understanding with all the other colonies to consider the British claims as a common cause to all, & to produce an unity of action."[61]

Though they became political rivals, Jefferson admired Patrick Henry's skill as an orator.

Marriage

Though Jefferson promoted free communication among the colonies, he was not skilled at some other forms of communication—as a young man, he was intensely shy around women. By his mid-twenties he had had only one serious infatuation, and that relationship ended at least partly because Jefferson was very clumsy in telling the young lady of his affection for her.

But then he met Martha Wayles Skelton, the widow of one of Jefferson's friends from William and Mary and the daughter of one of the richest planters in Virginia. One reason Jefferson was attracted to Martha was that she was also a great reader. Their interests especially coincided in their love for the novels of Laurence Sterne. They often read to one another and memorized favorite passages of the novels and many poems. Martha sang beautifully and played the harpsichord and spinet, which meant that she and Jefferson, still an avid

Jefferson and his future wife Martha found a common interest in the novels of Laurence Sterne (pictured).

violinist, could perform duets. Though for a while Martha's father thought Jefferson unworthy of her, the couple wore down all resistance during their two-year courtship. They were married on January 1, 1772.

The Declaration of Independence

Virginia chose Jefferson as a delegate to the Second Continental Congress, which reconvened in Philadelphia in September 1775. His fellow Virginians saw Jefferson as a patriot with strong opinions, especially after publication of his 1774 essay, "Summary View of the Rights of British America," which called for a firm political union of the colonies.

Congress adjourned in October 1775 but reconvened in May 1776 because there had been no response to its final appeal to the king for negotiations. On June 7, 1776, word reached Philadelphia that Virginia had declared independence. Whether Congress would follow suit was debated briefly, but some of the delegates refused to vote without consulting with their constituents. Before adjourning, Congress appointed a committee to draft a declaration of independence that the delegates could debate, revise, and vote on when they returned to Philadelphia.

Jefferson, Benjamin Franklin, and John Adams were among those chosen for the drafting committee. Though now regarded as one of the most important documents in American history, in his *Autobiography* Jefferson had almost nothing to say about his role in its creation: "The committee for drawing the declaration of Independence desired me to do it. It was accordingly done, and being approved by them, I reported it to the house on Friday the 28th of June."[62] Jefferson first submitted his draft to Franklin and then to Adams. Neither had exten- sive suggestions, but those they had were apparently incorporated into a second draft (the one Jefferson submitted on June 28, which has not survived).

After some debate, Congress voted on July 2, 1776, to declare independence from Great Britain. Then it was time to settle on the exact wording of the declaration.

Benjamin Franklin, Thomas Jefferson, John Adams, Robert Livingston, and Roger Sherman (left to right) draft the Declaration of Independence.

The draft of the Declaration of Independence Jefferson had submitted earlier was then debated and more revisions were made, some of them painful to Jefferson. One notable deletion was Jefferson's charge that the king was responsible for the slave trade. Though a slaveholder himself, Jefferson wanted the institution to end as soon as possible. But this section was deleted, first because the king could hardly be blamed for an institution participated in by thousands of colonists, and second because any provisions against slavery would be firmly opposed by delegates from the southern colonies.

Jefferson's revised declaration was finally approved on July 4. That night it was printed for distribution to the Continental army, the state legislatures, and the public.

Return to Virginia

Soon after the Declaration of Independence was promulgated, Jefferson declined a commission as a diplomat to France and resigned his seat in the Continental Congress so that he could be a member of the Virginia House of Delegates. Jefferson knew he was not a military man by training or inclination, and he was not yet ready to become a diplomat. He saw his duty as being first to his "country," Virginia, which was in the process of drafting a new constitution to enable it to function independently. While still in Philadelphia, Jefferson had written three versions of a constitution and sent them south. Though his proposals had little effect on decisions in Virginia at the time, Jefferson would later spend years working to get his ideas accepted.

Jefferson wanted to revise the laws of Virginia so that his state could make the transition from a British colony to independence. He thought that a revolution would be pointless if the new states did not devise a better plan of government than the one they had been living under. He wrote, "In truth, it is the whole object of the present controversy, for should a bad government be instituted for us in the future it had been as well to have accepted at first the bad one offered to us from beyond the water without the risk and expense of contest."[63]

His proposals, made first as a member of the Virginia House of Delegates and then as governor, were comprehensive and radical. According to Willard Sterne Randall, Jefferson proposed four major changes:

> repeal of the laws of entail and primogeniture [passing estates to the eldest son] that had built up a Tidewater aristocracy; establishing religious freedom; providing for "the more general diffusion of knowledge"—for the rest of his life he proselytized free public education—and streamlining Virginia's judiciary system while liberalizing her brutal penal code.[64]

A

SUMMARY VIEW

OF THE

RIGHTS

OF

BRITISH AMERICA.

SET FORTH IN SOME

RESOLUTIONS

INTENDED FOR THE

INSPECTION

OF THE PRESENT

DELEGATES

OF THE

PEOPLE OF VIRGINIA.

NOW IN

CONVENTION.

BY A NATIVE, AND MEMBER OF THE
HOUSE OF BURGESSES.
by Thomas Jefferson.

WILLIAMSBURG:
PRINTED BY CLEMENTINA RIND.

The title page of Jefferson's "Summary View of the Rights of British America," written in 1774.

Jefferson's proposals were considered too innovative by most of the other delegates to the Virginia Assembly. Many were never adopted, and some of those that were approved took many years to get through the legislature. But as Randall points out, the work Jefferson did "played a more critical role in . . . the creation of a commonwealth that was the forerunner of the federal government of the United States."[65]

Though Jefferson's disappointments over his legislative proposals had been great, a far larger test of his devotion to his state lay ahead.

Governor of Virginia

Despite the controversy that often swirled around him, Jefferson was a popular politician in Virginia and was selected by the legislature to two one-year terms as governor, serving from June 1779 to June 1781.

When Jefferson became governor, Virginia was in deep trouble on several fronts. The economy had been hurt by the war, the new state government had virtually no money, and there were no effective preparations to defend against British attacks. Randall explains that

As British armies marched and countermarched around New England and the Middle States and attacked Georgia and South Carolina, Virginia's eleven battalions of willing volunteers had been siphoned off by the

71

Continental Army, taking with them most of Virginia's usable firearms. Resupply from imperial French, Spanish, and Dutch trading partners on Caribbean islands had been all but stifled by an ever-tightening British navy blockade.[66]

The former governor, Patrick Henry, had been unable to improve the state's defenses. In fact, only a month before Jefferson took office a British raiding force had destroyed several towns by fire, carried off large quantities of arms and tobacco—Virginia's main cash crop—and taken well over one hundred boats. In the entire operation, lasting over two weeks, the British did not lose a single soldier.

Jefferson worked incessantly during his first year as governor to improve the situation. He tried several unsuccessful schemes to raise money for the government. He had better luck encouraging people to begin manufacturing goods that were hard to get from other sources because of the naval blockade, especially armaments. For example, he arranged for a cannon factory to be built inland, at what he hoped would be a safe distance from British raiding parties.

But the structure of the Virginia government made it difficult for him to get much accomplished. Though governor, he could do nothing without the consent of the eight-man Council of State, and he often had a hard time getting enough of

"I Tremble for My Country"

Though a slave owner himself, Jefferson thought slavery was morally wrong. He proposed legislation while in the Virginia House of Burgesses to limit slavery, and he spoke and wrote against the institution many times. In 1782 he wrote in *Notes on the State of Virginia* that slavery was damaging to master as well as slave.

> The whole commerce between master and slave is a perpetual exercise of the most boisterous passions, the most unremitting despotism on the one part, and degrading submissions on the other. Our children see this, and learn to imitate it. . . . The parent storms, the child looks on . . . and thus nursed, educated, and daily exercised in tyranny, cannot but be stamped by it with odious peculiarities.

Jefferson thought that eventually the slaves would rebel against their masters, and that God would be on the side of the slaves.

> Indeed I tremble for my country when I reflect that God is just: that his justice cannot sleep for ever: that considering numbers, nature and natural means only, a revolution of the wheel of fortune, an exchange of situation, is among possible events: that it may become probable by supernatural interference! The Almighty has no attribute which can take side with us in such a contest.

them together to make a quorum. Without the council he could not call out the militia or even appoint someone to a state job, but he was still held responsible for seeing that the laws of Virginia were carried out.

The British Attack

When sixty British ships carrying five thousand troops seized Hampton and Portsmouth in late 1780, Jefferson asked the Council of State to authorize a standing army, but they refused. By January 1781, the British were ready for an even bolder strike. Under the command of the American traitor Benedict Arnold, the British attempted to capture the capital city, Richmond, along with its stores of military supplies and tobacco—and Governor Thomas Jefferson. Arnold succeeded in burning and looting much of the town and even went upcountry to destroy the cannon factory, but he could not find Jefferson. After a few days he retired to Albemarle and fortified his position there.

Jefferson was in a nearly impossible situation as governor because following the British attack, several members of the Council of State had simply gone home to their plantations. Without a quorum, Jefferson was legally powerless. Nevertheless, he received a constant stream of requests for help from the towns. He was also under great strain personally because his wife and young daughter were both ill. His daughter died in April, and Jefferson was barely able to take a day away from his duties to comfort his wife and bury his child.

Command of the British forces was taken from Arnold and given to General Charles Cornwallis. Unable to gain a clear military victory, at the end of May 1781 Cornwallis decided to try again to capture Jefferson and members of the Council of State and the assembly, who were meeting at Charlottesville and nearby Monticello, Jefferson's home. Cornwallis sent a detachment under his most intrepid cavalry commander, Banastre Tarleton.

The British might have succeeded if it had not been for a Virginia militia officer who happened to be at an inn where Tarleton's corps took a rest break. The officer deduced Tarleton's mission and then rode forty miles nonstop to warn Jefferson and the others, who barely escaped. At that point Jefferson was not even the legal governor—his term had expired—but no replacement had been selected.

The thought of Jefferson fleeing from the British troubled some Virginia legislators, who accused him of failure to prepare for the attack and cowardice. They called for a formal inquiry. One was held, and Jefferson was cleared of any wrongdoing. His popularity in Virginia was damaged, but most people eventually realized that it would have been suicidal for Jefferson to have stayed to fight Tarleton and disastrous for morale if he had allowed himself to be captured.

Just four months after Tarleton's raid, the last major battle of the war took place in Virginia, at Yorktown. The formal end of the war would not be declared until September 1783, but Jefferson was able for a brief time to deal with more personal issues.

British commander Banastre Tarleton was unsuccessful in capturing Jefferson.

Among the Ashes

Though they failed to capture Jefferson, Tarleton and his men vandalized Monticello and burned Jefferson's crops, doing hundreds of thousands of dollars in damage. And of course during his service in the Continental Congress, in the Virginia legislature, and as governor, Jefferson had been unable to give much time to his plantation or to his law practice. His fi-

nancial problems were severe, and during his escape from Monticello he had been injured in a fall from his horse. His recuperation gave him a chance to work in his library and write the only book of his to be published during his lifetime, *Notes on the State of Virginia.*

Jefferson's wife Martha died in September 1782. Martha asked him not to remarry, not wanting their daughters to have to submit to a stepmother, and Jefferson kept his promise. He was deeply depressed for months following his wife's death, and he was left with the sole responsibility for raising their three surviving children, Patsy, Polly, and Lucy Elizabeth.

Jefferson was elected to Congress in June 1783. He was made a member of most of the important committees and drafted thirty state papers (proposals for government policies). Several of these have had lasting implications, among them "Notes on the Establishment of a Money Unit," which outlined the system of decimal coinage still in use in the United States. But life in Congress, with its seemingly endless debates, did not suit him.

Ambassador and Politician

In May 1784 Jefferson was appointed to work with Benjamin Franklin and John Adams on establishing trade relations with sixteen European countries. After extensive preparations, including a tour of several states Jefferson had never visited before, he and his daughter Patsy sailed for France, arriving in Paris in August. He would stay in Europe for five years.

Jefferson succeeded Franklin as ambassador to France in 1785. With the help of his old friend the Marquis de Lafayette, he negotiated improvements in trade relations with France. He also had great success in working out a treaty with Prussia—the king of Prussia was very impressed with Jefferson—and in 1785 he went to London to work with John Adams on improving trade relations with Britain. They were not able to make much

progress, but they toured the English countryside together, giving Jefferson a chance to study English gardens and mechanical inventions. In 1787 Jefferson toured Italy. He was surprised by the productivity of Italian rice farming, and he smuggled out rice seeds for experimental use in the United States, an offense which carried the death penalty.

Jefferson returned to the United States in 1789 and in March 1790 became secretary of state in the Washington administration. Jefferson's years in that position were marred by his intense rivalry with Alexander Hamilton, the secretary of the treasury. Jefferson thought Hamilton wanted to make the federal government too powerful,

Jefferson and Money

Thomas Jefferson had problems with money most of his adult life. Some were beyond his control; others were of his own making. He has often been criticized for buying more books, scientific instruments, violins, and bottles of wine than he could afford. He also spent lavishly on building his main house, Monticello, and a nearby summer house.

Other money problems were simply hazards of the time. For example, in those days there were no rural fire departments or homeowner's insurance—in February 1770 his family's home at Shadwell, where he and his mother still lived, was destroyed by fire. Jefferson lost almost all his books, including his expensive law books, and the records of his legal practice. The books alone were worth over $20,000 in today's money.

Three years later Jefferson's father-in-law, John Wayles, died and left a third of his sizable estate to Martha and thus to Jefferson. On paper, Wayles's property was worth about twice his debts, but his debts had to be paid in cash, of which there was very little in colonial Virginia. Jefferson tried to pay the debts by selling land, but he had to take notes (installment agreements) for much of the selling price. When Virginia declared independence in 1776, it started issuing its own money, which the buyers used to pay Jefferson. Unfortunately, during the war the paper money became almost worthless, and Jefferson was left with a huge debt that he was never able to repay.

Finally, Jefferson lost perhaps $300,000 in today's money when Monticello and his crops were vandalized by marauding British troops in 1781. The result of all this was that when Jefferson died in 1826, his debts were so large that Monticello had to be sold.

decreasing individual liberties. Hamilton thought Jefferson was merely a political theorist whose ideas would leave government too weak to help the people. Washington tried to steer a course between these two points of view, but in general Hamilton's proposals prevailed. Jefferson resigned in December 1793.

Jefferson had three years of relative retirement from politics between late 1793 and late 1796, though he was in close touch with his friend James Madison, who was then a leading member of the House of Representatives. George Washington declined to run for a third term as president in 1796, and in the balloting that year John Adams received the most votes, with Jefferson second, making him the new vice president. (Before passage of the Twelfth Amendment in 1804, the second-highest vote getter for president was named vice president.)

During their service together in Washington's first administration, Jefferson had become increasingly alienated from Adams, who had been one of his closest friends just a few years before. There was concern after the election that Jefferson would refuse to be vice president under Adams, but Jefferson thought that Adams might make a good president after all, and in any case the job of vice president had few duties, allowing Jefferson to pursue his other interests. Adams and Jefferson both tried to work together in the early days of their administration, but their relationship soon broke down.

Their animosity even contributed to a national crisis. In 1798, war with France threatened, and with Adams's support Congress passed four laws known as the Alien and Sedition Acts. Three of these concerned recent immigrants who might have sided with France if war broke out. The fourth, though, the Sedition Act, was clearly aimed at Jefferson and other critics of Adams. It provided for jail sentences for anyone who published articles critical of Adams's policies or acts of Congress, and because it automatically expired in 1800, it also seemed designed to stifle criticism of Adams during the upcoming presidential election.

Jefferson led the opposition to the Alien and Sedition Acts, though he was forced to do it secretly. Protests erupted in many areas of the country, and the laws damaged Adams politically much more than they helped him. In the election of 1800, one of the most heated campaigns in American history, Adams lost to Jefferson.

President

Many historians consider the high point of Jefferson's presidency the Louisiana Purchase of 1803, in which France sold the United States its North American territories for $15 million. The deal doubled the size of the United States overnight and opened up a vast new area for exploration and expansion.

Jefferson was reelected in 1804. He thought that the new territories gained

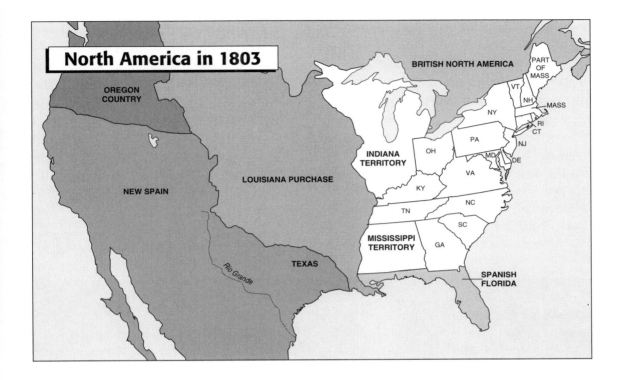

from the French should be explored, and so he supported the Lewis and Clark expedition up the Missouri River and on to the Pacific (1804–1806) and the expeditions of Zebulon Pike to the headwaters of the Mississippi River and the southern Rocky Mountains (1806–1807). He also used U.S. naval power to fight against the Barbary pirates, North African raiders who captured American ships and held their passengers hostage.

Jefferson declined to run for a third term as president, and his good friend James Madison was elected. Jefferson looked forward to returning to Monticello and having at least a few years to be with his family, to farm, to study, and to repair his shattered finances.

Retirement

Three themes dominated Jefferson's final years: friendship, education, and money.

John Adams had been Jefferson's collaborator and close friend for many years before their differing views of the proper role of government in the new United States drove them apart in the 1790s. Even after their split, and the political divisions that accompanied it, they still had mutual friends. One of those, Dr. Benjamin Rush, worked tirelessly to get them back together. Rush corresponded frequently with each of them and would include news of the other in his letters. After many hints that they should write to one another, Rush stretched the truth a bit and told Adams that Jefferson would welcome a renewal of their friendship. Adams wrote Jefferson and, luckily for Rush, Jefferson responded warmly. This was the beginning of an exchange of letters over a vast range of subjects—personal, political, philosophical, and scientific—that continued until their final days. It was obvious to all who knew him that

patching up his relationship with Adams made the other difficulties in Jefferson's life much easier to deal with.

Education had been one of Jefferson's prime concerns for decades. He advocated free public education at a time when the idea was still considered radical, and he had no luck getting the Virginia legislature to go along with him in the early days of independence. But

Thomas Jefferson selected the site and designed some of the buildings of the University of Virginia.

Thomas Jefferson and Sally Hemings

No controversy involving a Revolutionary leader has been as durable nor as heated as the question of whether Jefferson fathered some or all of the children of one of his slaves, Sally Hemings. Hemings had come to Monticello from the estate of Martha Jefferson's father after his death in 1773 and has been thought to be Martha's half-sister, having been fathered by John Wayles. Sally Hemings was reportedly very beautiful.

The charge that Jefferson was the father of Hemings's children became public in the election campaign of 1800. Until very recently, most of Jefferson's biographers dismissed as preposterous the idea that he could have had a sexual relationship with a slave. Hemings's descendants, however, cited the recollections of their ancestors that Sally's children were very fair-skinned, some of them entering white society, and that it was common knowledge in the Jefferson household that Thomas Jefferson was their father.

In 1998, DNA samples were taken from members of the Hemings and Jefferson families. At first the results were taken to mean that Jefferson was definitely the father of Sally Hemings's children. Then others pointed out that the results could indicate that some other member of Jefferson's family might have been the father. The question may never be settled.

in retirement Jefferson thought that he could have the greatest influence on education in his state by founding a new university, which he hoped would become the finest in the nation. Beginning work in 1814 to convince Virginia officials that the state should have a university, by 1819 the University of Virginia was under construction. Jefferson chose the site (he could see it with a telescope from Monticello), designed the buildings, and headed its governing council.

Unfortunately, Jefferson was never able to recover from the financial losses he suffered during the Revolutionary War and the neglect of his business affairs necessitated by forty years of public service. This was his greatest worry during his retirement. Though he and his friends tried several schemes to raise money for him, in his last years he knew

that he would leave his heirs debts of well over $100,000.

Legacy

Ten days before his death, in turning down an invitation to the celebration in Washington of the fiftieth anniversary of the Declaration of Independence, Jefferson wrote,

I should, indeed, with peculiar delight, have met and exchanged there congratulations personally with the small band, the remnant of that host of worthies, who joined with us on that day [July 4, 1776], in the bold and doubtful election we were to make for our country, between submission or the sword; and to have enjoyed with them the consolatory fact, that our fellow citizens, after half a century of experience and prosperity, continue to approve the choice we made.[67]

Like his friend John Adams, Jefferson seemed to struggle to stay alive until July 4. He succeeded, dying about noon that day. Though he had been a legislator, ambassador, secretary of state, vice president, and president, Jefferson directed that only three achievements be listed on his headstone: writing the Declaration of Independence, drafting the Virginia Statute of Religious Toleration, and founding the University of Virginia.

Alexander Hamilton

Alexander Hamilton was one of the most controversial figures of the Revolutionary era. He was an effective political writer before the war, advocating a break with Britain. Ambitious for fame and honor, he became an artillery commander early in the war and was soon widely known for his courage and daring. He then became one of General George Washington's assistants. In fact, he became nearly indispensable to Washington, developing a relationship that was almost like that of father and son.

Many historians have seen in his politics reflections of a childhood full of loss and insecurity. He felt that the most legitimate branch of government was the executive because the president could act as a loving and protective father. Hamilton wanted his country to devise the best possible system of government, above all, one that was honest and concerned for its people. He was afraid that the states would be governed by men acting in favor of local interests, so he wanted a strong central government that would act for the benefit of the whole nation.

Childhood

Alexander Hamilton's mother was Rachel Faucett Lavien, about whom little is known for certain. In 1745 Rachel married a planter named Johann Lavien, probably on the Caribbean island of St. Croix. They had a son, Peter, but their marriage was not happy. Rachel left Johann in 1750, and he had her jailed for it. She won her release and moved to the island of St. Kitts, but Lavien refused to give her a divorce.

By 1752 Rachel was living on the island of Nevis with James Hamilton, a Scottish merchant. He came from a wealthy family but had difficulty making a living. Their son James was born in 1753, and Alexander was born January 11, 1757. Lavien finally divorced Rachel in 1759, but the decree prohibited her remarriage.

Alexander Hamilton advocated a strong central government for America.

Then Rachel died in 1768. Lavien, her former husband, objected to her will because it left her meager property to her illegitimate sons James and Alexander. The court awarded all of her property to her one legitimate son, Peter. Alexander was taken in by members of his mother's family, James and Peter Lytton. He went to work in a store on St. Croix in 1769. But there was still no stability or security in his life: Both James and Peter Lytton died that summer.

Despite all the death and disruption in his young life, Hamilton does not seem to have become depressed or hopeless. Instead he was eager to show the world what he could accomplish. In his earliest surviving letter, written in November 1769 to his friend Ned Stevens, Hamilton makes clear that the little island and his life as a clerk were not going to be enough for him, and his special hope was for a chance to prove himself in battle:

James Hamilton, Rachel, and their sons moved to the island of St. Croix in 1765. James continued to have business difficulties, and in 1766 he left his family and never returned.

> Ned, my Ambition is prevalent that I . . . would willingly risk my life tho' not my Character to exalt my Station.

Im confident, Ned that my Youth excludes me from any hopes of immediate Preferment nor do I desire it, but I mean to prepare the way for futurity. Im no Philosopher you see and may be jusly said to Build Castles in the Air. . . . [Y]et Neddy we have seen such Schemes successfull when the Projector is Constant I shall Conclude saying I wish there was a War.[68]

Storm-Blown to New York

Hamilton would become the most prolific journalist among the founders, and his career as a writer began early. In October 1772, when he was only fifteen, his account of a hurricane was published in the *Royal Danish American Gazette*:

Good God! what horror and destruction. Its impossible for me to describe or you to form any idea of it. It seemed as if a total dissolution of nature was taking place. The roaring of the sea and wind, fiery meteors flying about it in the air, the prodigious

Alexander Hamilton was born in 1757 in this Charlestown, Nevis house in the West Indies.

glare of almost perpetual lightning, the crash of the falling houses, and the ear-splitting shrieks of the distressed, were sufficient to strike astonishment into Angels.[69]

The hurricane and Hamilton's account of it proved pivotal for him. He had already been noticed for his exceptional intelligence by Hugh Knox, a Presbyterian minister who thought that opportunities for education should be given to any poor person who was likely to benefit. Hamilton was also highly thought of by his employer, Nicholas Cruger. Together Knox and Cruger used the emotions stirred up by the devastation of the hurricane and Hamilton's article to raise the money needed to send him to college in America.

College

Exactly when Hamilton arrived in New York is disputed. Some say it was in the late fall of 1772, but it was no later than June 1773. He was under the sponsorship of two friends of Hugh Knox: Elias Boudinot, a prominent attorney who would later become president of the Continental Congress, and William Livingston, another attorney who would become the first governor of New Jersey after independence was declared in 1776.

Hamilton was first enrolled at a Presbyterian academy in Elizabethtown, New

An educational sponsor, Elias Boudinot is best known as president of the Continental Congress.

Jersey, where he studied Latin and Greek. After a few months there he applied to Myles Cooper, the president of King's College (now Columbia University), and was admitted as a special student. Hamilton was so successful in his first year there that he was made a regular student in 1774. Hamilton's life had undergone a tremendous change. Not long before he had been an impoverished, parentless boy on a small Caribbean island. Now, with the help of a few generous friends who had confidence in his potential, Hamilton was a student at a fine college and the protégé of wealthy and influential men who could guide and promote his career.

Young Politician

Hamilton's career as a political writer began while he was still in college with several pro-revolution pamphlets written in 1774 and 1775. One of the first was "A Full Vindication of the Measures of the Congress," which was his response to an article by Samuel Seabury, an Anglican priest and physician who had written that he would not comply with measures passed by the new Continental Congress to stop trading with Great Britain. Hamilton responded that Congress should be respected because its members were honorable citizens elected by their colonies to perform important duties. Hamilton insisted that what Congress had done was sound and that it was up to the people to make it work.

Young Hero

Alexander Hamilton exhibited his courage and gallantry even before he began his military career. One night Myles Cooper, the president of King's College, was threatened by a mob of overenthusiastic patriots because Cooper was a British loyalist. Hamilton stood on Cooper's doorstep and yelled at the crowd not to dishonor the cause of liberty by violence against Cooper. The crowd was not completely persuaded by Hamilton's speech, but they were delayed long enough for Cooper to leave by a backdoor and seek safety on a British warship.

In this early pamphlet Hamilton also sounded one of the clarion calls of the Revolution, that the American colonies had no responsibility to obey the British House of Commons, in which they had no representatives:

What then is the subject of our controversy with the mother country? It is this, whether we shall preserve that security to our lives and properties, which the law of nature, the genius of the British constitution, and our charters afford us; or whether we shall resign them into the hands of the British House of Commons, which is no more privileged to dispose of them than the Grand Mogul?[70]

It was significant that, unlike most political authors of the time, who wrote as citizens of a particular colony, Hamilton wrote as an American. Because he was a recent immigrant from the Caribbean, he had no strong ties to any individual colony, but he had become deeply committed to the emerging nation.

Captain of Artillery

Hamilton's education was cut short by his desire for glory on the battlefield. In 1775 he began drilling with a company of volunteers that called themselves the Corsicans. They wore leather caps with the words "Liberty or Death" on them. Though they were not part of the army, they nevertheless decided to deprive the British of some of their armaments. According to biographer Richard Brookhiser,

> At the end of August 1775, the young soldiers went to the [New York] Battery to remove its cannons. [Hamilton's friend Hercules] Mulligan, who went with them, remembered that "Mr. H[amilton] . . . gave me his musket to hold" and grabbed one of the cannon ropes. A British battleship in the harbor opened fire on them. "I left his musket in the Battery & retreated." Hamilton retreated with his cannon, and asked Mulligan for his musket. When told that it was back at the fort, "he went for it . . . with as much unconcern as if the vessel had not been there."[71]

In March 1776 Hamilton was made a captain of artillery in the Provincial Com-

pany of New York. Hamilton was responsible for recruiting men for his unit, and at that time New York did not provide uniforms for its troops. To make serving in the army more attractive, Hamilton bought uniforms for his men, the cost to be deducted from their pay. So that he would be technically proficient when a chance for battle actually arose, he studied gunnery.

Hamilton got his chance in August 1776 when he was commander of artillery in the Battle of Long Island, New York, in which the British forced Washington to retreat. Hamilton also participated in battles at Princeton and Trenton in New Jersey late in 1776. According to biographer Noemie Emery:

> One officer saw his [Hamilton's] company marching into Princeton. "It was a model of discipline, at their head was a boy, and I wondered at his youth, but what was my surprise when he was pointed out to me as that Hamilton of whom we had heard so much." He was living his fantasies, as were others of Washington's young troops.[72]

Though he was frequently ill while in the army and unable to attend to his duties, he was recognized as one who pushed himself to extremes and would dare anything to advance the cause of the Revolution. According to Emery:

> At twenty-two, he had evolved a code of honor that would control him all

Hamilton participated in the Battle of Long Island where the British forced Washington's army to retreat.

his life. He took the great for models, tried to emulate them and lashed himself severely when he failed. His heroes were soldiers and statesmen, sometimes both, who found their private joy in public service and placed cause and country above self. Their gods were *civitas* [citizenship] and honor—intense pride in private excellence and absolute devotion to the state. There was the implicit embrace of danger: few of his heroes died quietly in bed. There was also the acceptance of a deadly bargain: life was the coin with which to purchase fame.[73]

Impressed with Hamilton's performance in battle, General Nathaniel Greene introduced him to Washington. Washington was immediately impressed with the young artillery commander, but more with his intellect and facility with words than with his military skill. Washington invited Hamilton to join his headquarters staff. Hamilton reluctantly agreed. He would have preferred to stay in the field, but few could refuse a request from Washington. Hamilton became Washington's secretary and aide de camp (ADC) in March 1777.

Hamilton and Washington

Washington soon developed tremendous confidence in Hamilton. In late October 1777 Washington's army was deadlocked with the British at Philadelphia. He and his staff decided to send a representative north to General Horatio Gates to determine whether a brigade could be detached from his force and sent to join Washington. The commander in chief chose Hamilton for the mission. According to historian Broadus Mitchell, Hamilton "was to decide whether the war was to be prosecuted in the north or in the region of Philadelphia."[74] Hamilton judged that a brigade could be sent south, but Gates tried to dispatch one that was under strength. Hamilton learned of this, perhaps from a friend on Gates's staff. The twenty-year-old ADC demanded a full brigade. General Gates complied.

Hamilton was known for his military bearing and for his wit, kindness, and the depth of his political convictions. George Washington, who was childless, called his headquarters staff "the family," thinking of the other senior officers as brothers and the aides as his sons. More than the other aides, Hamilton, who had been abandoned by his father, was truly like a son to Washington. Hamilton seemed to know what Washington wanted to say with little explanation, and so the general gave him the job of drafting official correspondence.

Hamilton was staunchly loyal when others criticized Washington. In December 1778, General Charles Lee, who was awaiting trial on charges of cowardice, slandered Washington to other officers. Hamilton challenged Lee to a duel, but his friend John Laurens, another of Washington's aides, had done so first. Hamilton served as Laurens's second. Lee was wounded by Laurens's first shot, and Hamilton and the other second intervened to stop the duel. Hamilton's challenge to Lee again showed that for him, life without honor was worthless.

Hamilton had fulfilled many of his early ambitions. Two remained for him to pursue: He wanted to command troops in battle, and he wanted to start a family.

Courtship

In a half-joking letter to John Laurens in April 1779 Hamilton said of his ideal wife,

> She must be young, handsome (I lay most stress upon a good shape) sensible (a little learning will do), well bred . . . chaste and tender (I am an enthusiast in my notions of fidelity and fondness) of some good nature, a great deal of generosity (she must

love neither money nor scolding . . .). In politics I am indifferent what side she may be of; I think I have arguments that will easily convert her to mine. As to religion a moderate stock will satisfy me. . . . But as to fortune, the larger stock of that the better. . . . As I have not much of my own and as I am very little calculated to get more either by my address or industry; it must need be that my wife, if I get one, bring at least a sufficiency to administer to her own extravagancies.[75]

Hamilton soon met someone who met all of those requirements. Elizabeth Schuyler was the daughter of Philip Schuyler, who had recently resigned his commission as a general in the Continental army and was then a member of Congress for New York. The Schuyler family was one of the wealthiest in the colonies, so Elizabeth was accustomed to comfort and luxury. Hamilton was poor and not especially interested in becoming rich. He warned Elizabeth repeatedly that she might face a life of poverty, but she was undeterred. They were married on December 14, 1780, and he was essentially adopted into the Schuyler family. Hamilton at last had the security and support that had been denied him in his childhood.

The Arnold Treason

Hamilton was with Washington on an inspection tour of West Point on September 25, 1780, when the plot of General Benedict Arnold to assist the British in capturing the fort was discovered. After Arnold escaped from West Point, his wife, Peggy Shippen Arnold, seemed to be nearly mad with worry and grief. Hamilton was sympathetic to her, writing to Elizabeth that "Her sufferings were so eloquent that I wished myself her brother, to have a right to become her defender."[76] It was later discovered that she had been a co-conspirator with her husband. This is an early example of Hamilton's tendency to come to the aid of women who seemed to be in distress, which would later prove nearly disastrous for him.

Benedict Arnold's treason was discovered when a British officer, Major John André, was captured carrying incriminating documents. André was out of uniform at the time and so was being treated as a spy, which meant that he was to be executed by hanging rather than a firing squad. André, a gallant and highly respected officer, asked Washington for the firing squad, which was considered a more honorable death. Hamilton pleaded with Washington to grant André's request; Washington refused. Hamilton wrote to Elizabeth that Washington was "only sensible to motives of policy" and that his refusal of André's request would eventually "be branded with too much obduracy [stubbornness]."[77]

Falling Out with Washington

In February 1781 an incident occurred at headquarters that severely tested one

General Benedict Arnold (left) commits treason by sharing information with the British.

of Hamilton's primary relationships. He wrote about it to his father-in-law:

[A]n unexpected change has taken place in my situation. I am no longer a member of the General's family. . . . Two day[s] ago The General and I passed each other on the stairs. He told me he wanted to speak to me. I answered that I would wait upon him immediately. I went down below and delivered Mr. Tilghman [another ADC] a letter. . . . Returning to The General I was stopped in the way by the Marquis De la Fayette, and we conversed together about a minute on a matter of business. . . . Instead of finding the General as usual in his room, I met him at the head of the stairs, where accosting me in a very angry tone, "Col Hamilton (said he), you have kept me waiting at the head of the stairs these ten minutes. I must tell you Sir you treat me with disrespect." I replied without petulancy, but with decision "I am not conscious of it Sir, but since you have thought it necessary to tell me so we part." "Very well Sir (said he) if it be your choice."[78]

Hamilton submitted his resignation from Washington's staff, saying that he would stay until a replacement could be found. Washington made overtures to patch up the rift, but Hamilton rejected them. And despite having promised Washington to keep the quarrel secret, Hamilton wrote to several friends about it.

Washington's unwillingness to give Hamilton a field command surely was a factor in Hamilton's overreaction to their disagreement. But Washington had a sound military reason—military units in the Revolution were made up of men from one area who wanted officers whom they knew. Units had even rioted when given outsiders to command them. Perhaps Washington's denial of André's request also contributed to Hamilton's dissatisfaction, but again, Washington had sound reasons for his actions.

Hamilton the Commander

Despite their strained relationship, Hamilton continued to press Washington for a field command. Eventually Hamilton threatened to leave the army entirely if not given one, and Washington granted his request. Hamilton was made commander of a light infantry unit and sent south to Yorktown, Virginia.

Hamilton was overjoyed at having a field command, and his exuberance almost got the better of him. During the siege of Yorktown Hamilton's troops were the first to occupy a trench dug to provide the American army a safe place from which to fire its cannons. As Hamilton's men marched into the trench, the British artillery fired at them, to no effect. Hamilton may have felt the protection his troops received from the trench was not quite honorable, because he then ordered his men onto the open field. Though they were completely exposed to the British positions, he had them perform the manual of arms before returning to the trench. The British did not fire a shot during this exercise, perhaps because they were too astonished at Hamilton's daring.

Not long after this incident, on the night of October 14, 1781, Hamilton commanded his unit in an attack on a British fortification. The battle only lasted about ten minutes, but the attack was successful and it gave Hamilton the chance to prove his bravery in battle. As it happened, Yorktown was the last major engagement of the war.

In late 1781 Hamilton asked to be furloughed. There seemed to be little chance of further military action, and he knew that the work of building the new nation was just beginning. In 1781 and 1782, even before the formal end of the war, Hamilton wrote anonymous newspaper articles known as the Continentalist

Letters, which advocated a strong central government. This was a theme he would continue to advance the rest of his life.

Lawyer and Politician

Soon after Hamilton left the army he began to study law under his friend Robert Troup, who lived with the Hamiltons while serving as tutor. Hamilton was admitted to the New York bar in July 1782 after only six months of intense study. His law practice was successful, but he tended to charge less than other lawyers and would defend clients for no fee at all if he thought their case had merit.

In September 1786 Hamilton was sent by the New York legislature to a conference on interstate commerce held in Annapolis, Maryland. Only eleven other delegates from five states attended, but before adjourning they adopted a resolution, drafted by Hamilton, calling for a convention to meet in May 1787 to revise the Articles of Confederation.

Hamilton was one of New York's delegates to the Constitutional Convention. His only speech to the convention was re-

Hamilton left the military in 1781 to study law under his friend Robert Troup.

garded as ill-considered even by some of his friends. He praised the British system, saying that the hereditary monarchy resulted in a convergence of interests between king and people, and that the House of Lords was a good check on both the monarch and the House of Commons. For America, he suggested a life term during good behavior and a high salary for the president as deterrents to corruption. The monarchist tone of his speech would be used against him by his enemies for years to come.

Hamilton was deeply frustrated at the convention. His vote was meaningless because each of the states voted as a unit, and the other two New York delegates consistently opposed Hamilton's views. He left the convention early, convinced that he could have no influence on the outcome, and only returned after the major issues had been settled.

Though Hamilton was ineffective at the convention and disliked many of the provisions of the constitution it wrote, he had a key role in ratifying it. He thought the constitution would be too weak to control unruly human passions, but if it was rejected Hamilton feared even more the consequences of continuing under the Articles of Confederation.

At Hamilton's instigation, between October 1787 and May 1788 he and his friends James Madison and John Jay wrote a series of eighty-five articles in defense of the constitution, later collected in book form under the title *The Federalist*. Hamilton wrote about fifty of the articles, which were addressed to the people of New York, a crucial state in the ratification process. Hamilton's contributions

Alexander Hamilton, James Madison, and John Jay (pictured) authored The Federalist *detailing the purposes of American government.*

to *The Federalist* were a lengthy and detailed statement of his convictions regarding the purposes of government.

Thanks in part to Hamilton's efforts, New York approved the new Constitution. When he returned to New York City from the ratification convention in July 1788 he was given a parade and treated like a hero.

Secretary of the Treasury

By 1789 Hamilton and Washington had resumed their cordial working relationship. In September the Department of the Treasury was approved by Congress and Hamilton was appointed its first secretary. He would hold the office until January 1795. After the presidency, it was perhaps the most difficult job in the government and the most important. The new Constitution made the old way of conducting the government's affairs obsolete, and a new system had to be devised. Hamilton's challenges were tremendous. He had to propose new institutions and procedures; argue for their acceptance by Washing-

President Washington consults with cabinet members, Thomas Jefferson (left) and Alexander Hamilton (center).

ton, other members of the cabinet, and Congress; and then put them into effect.

In his years at the treasury, Hamilton established a system for public credit, formed the Bank of the United States, helped resolve the complex issue of the war debts of the states, carried on unofficial negotiations with Great Britain to improve trade relations, and established accounting and other procedures for the department. In 1794, Hamilton and Washington put down a massive and potentially violent tax protest in western Pennsylvania known as the Whiskey Rebellion.

None of Hamilton's goals were accomplished without opposition, some of it from within the cabinet. Thomas Jefferson, then secretary of state, urged others to write newspaper articles critical of Hamilton on several issues, and Jefferson was later responsible for resolutions in Congress questioning and then condemning his conduct in office. Hamilton responded to all of these attacks by writing his own articles defending his actions and calling for a congressional investigation of his department. In the end he was cleared of any misconduct, but the constant battles were upsetting to him and contributed to his decision to resign as secretary of the treasury.

The Reynolds Affair

Hamilton's political life was full of controversy, but his greatest public humiliation came over his relationship with a woman who, like Peggy Arnold, seemed to have been abandoned.

Hamilton, whose own mother had been abused and abandoned, was always sympathetic to the plight of women in distress. In July 1791 Hamilton was approached by Mrs. Maria Reynolds, who said she had been deserted by her husband and wanted to borrow money so that she could return to her family. Hamilton agreed and arranged to meet her later that day. Several years later he wrote that he went to Mrs. Reynolds's

Farewell to His Wife

At the time of his death, Hamilton had mended his relationship with his wife and was close to his children, trying his best to be a good father. The anguish he felt at the prospect of leaving his family is expressed in a letter to his wife written July 4, 1804. The letter is in Hamilton's *Writings*, edited by Joanne B. Freeman.

This letter, my very dear Eliza, will not be delivered to you, unless I shall first have terminated my earthly career; to begin, as I humbly hope from redeeming grace and divine mercy, a happy immortality.

If it had been possible for me to have avoided this interview [the duel], my love for you and my precious children would have been alone a decisive motive. But it was not possible, without sacrifices which would have rendered me unworthy of your esteem. I need not tell you of the pangs I feel, from the idea of quitting you and exposing you to the anguish which I know you would feel. Nor could I dwell on the topic lest it should unman me.

The consolations of Religion, my beloved, can alone support you; and these you have a right to enjoy. Fly to the bosom of your God and be comforted. With my last idea; I shall cherish the sweet hope of meeting you in a better world.

Adieu best of wives and best of Women. Embrace all my darling Children for me.

Ever yours
AH

rooming house and was shown up to her bedroom. After he offered her the money she had asked for, "Some conversation ensued from which it was quickly apparent that other than pecuniary consolation would be acceptable."[79]

Hamilton had an affair with Maria Reynolds, but it later became known that Maria and her husband had planned to get money from Hamilton, first on the pretext that she had been abandoned, and then as blackmail both regarding the affair and over false allegations of misconduct as secretary of the treasury.

The Reynolds's plot first came to light in 1792 when Reynolds and another man were arrested. They tried to escape prosecution by accusing Hamilton of illegal financial speculation. Approached by a congressional delegation, Hamilton quickly established that although he had had an affair with Maria, he had not done anything illegal. He thought the matter was settled until it came up again five years later in an article by muckraking journalist James Callender. Hamilton soon produced a pamphlet explaining the entire case, with copies of supporting documents. His wife stood by him through the crisis. Though the affair provided ammunition for his critics, it did not seem to diminish his public esteem or Washington's opinion of his abilities.

Inspector General

Hamilton worked against the election of John Adams in 1796, and they were bitter enemies. When war with France seemed imminent in 1798, President Adams asked George Washington to head a new army that would have to be recruited, trained, and led. Washington agreed on the condition that he have complete freedom to choose his staff, and he wanted Hamilton to be second in command. Adams tried to make Hamilton fourth in command; Washington threatened to resign. He wrote to Adams of Hamilton:

> By some he is considered as an ambitious man, and therefore a dangerous one. That he is ambitious I shall readily grant, but it is of that laudable kind which prompts a man to excel in whatever he takes in hand. He is enterprising, quick in his perceptions, and his judgment intuitively great: qualities essential to a Military character, and therefore I repeat, that his loss will be irreparable.[80]

Adams backed down, and Hamilton was made inspector general of the army. Some feared that Hamilton would use his new position to begin an aggressive war to take Louisiana from France and Mexico from Spain. However, before the army could be raised, the crisis with France was resolved.

Over the next few years Hamilton faced several personal losses. Both James Hamilton and George Washington died in 1799. In November 1801 Hamilton's elder son, Philip, died following a duel in which

The Hamilton-Knox-Burr Connection

Alexander Hamilton's connections with Vice President Aaron Burr, the man who killed him in a duel in 1804, had an odd beginning. Hamilton's friend and sponsor on St. Croix, the Rev. Hugh Knox, had studied at the College of New Jersey (now Princeton University). The head of the college was Aaron Burr Sr., the father of the future vice president. Hugh Knox stayed at the college an extra year after graduation, studying theology with the elder Burr, and so was almost like a member of the Burr family.

In 1799 Hamilton's brother-in-law, John Church, met Burr at Weehawken for a duel in which neither man was injured. Then in 1801 Hamilton's son Philip was killed in a duel by George Eaker, a supporter of Aaron Burr. Their argument stemmed from a speech Eaker had made that criticized Philip's father. The pistols used in both of these duels were the same ones Hamilton and Burr later used.

Aaron Burr and Alexander Hamilton duel.

he was defending his father's honor. As a result of Philip's death, Hamilton's daughter Angelica had a nervous breakdown from which she never recovered.

Many of Hamilton's friends believed that he never fully recovered from these traumas, either. Hamilton had always had a bleak view of life. Twenty years earlier he had written to his friend John Laurens, "I am disgusted with every thing in this world but yourself and *very* few more honest fellows and I have no other wish than as soon as possible to make a brilliant exit."[81] In 1804 he was to do just that.

The Interview at Weehawken

On June 18, 1804, Vice President Aaron Burr wrote to Hamilton demanding an explanation of a published letter by Dr. Charles Cooper saying that Hamilton had publicly characterized Burr's actions as "despicable." Burr wanted either an apology or a duel. But Cooper had not specified exactly what Hamilton had said. Hamilton responded that he could not be held to account for everything he had said about Burr over the preceding fifteen years. Burr would not relent. He seized on Hamilton's admission that he had criticized Burr at various times for fifteen years and demanded a complete apology. Hamilton refused, and so a duel was arranged. It took place on July 11, 1804, near Weehawken, New Jersey.

Dueling was illegal in most states. It was still practiced, however, with precau-

tions such as calling the duel itself an "interview." The duel between Hamilton and Burr continues to be debated by scholars. Most duels did not result in death or serious injury to either party. It is likely that neither Burr nor Hamilton intended to shoot the other. One reconstruction of the duel has Hamilton firing first, but intentionally high and into a tree behind Burr, severing a branch. Then Burr fired, possibly aiming at Hamilton's leg, a wound that would have stopped the duel. His bullet struck Hamilton's lower abdomen, however, deflected off his hip bone, and went through his liver, causing internal bleeding that led to Hamilton's death the next day.

Burr was charged with murder, fled the city, and his political career was ruined. Hamilton was given a hero's funeral. The City of New York asked all businesses to close that day and churches to ring muffled bells. His friends raised money to pay his debts and help raise his children, and Elizabeth, who lived another fifty years, "devoted herself to gathering his papers, which are the memorials of his greatness."[82]

★ Notes ★

Introduction

1. Quoted in A.J. Langguth, *Patriots: The Men Who Started the American Revolution.* New York: Simon and Schuster, 1988, p. 208.
2. Quoted in David McCullough, *John Adams.* New York: Simon and Schuster, 2001, p. 86.

Chapter 1: Benjamin Franklin

3. Benjamin Franklin, *Autobiography, Poor Richard, and Later Writings,* ed. J.A. Leo Lemay. New York: Library of America, 1997, p. 585.
4. Quoted in Esmond Wright, *Benjamin Franklin: His Life as He Wrote It.* Cambridge, MA: Harvard University Press, 1989, pp. 76–77.
5. Franklin, *Autobiography, Poor Richard, and Later Writings,* p. 631.
6. Franklin, *Autobiography, Poor Richard, and Later Writings,* p. 667.
7. Franklin, *Autobiography, Poor Richard, and Later Writings,* p. 621.
8. Franklin, *Autobiography, Poor Richard, and Later Writings,* p. 640.
9. Quoted in Wright, *Benjamin Franklin,* pp. 130–31.
10. Quoted in Wright, *Benjamin Franklin,* p. 177.
11. Quoted in Wright, *Benjamin Franklin,* p. 274.
12. Quoted in Wright, *Benjamin Franklin,* p. 274.

Chapter 2: Paul Revere

13. Henry Steele Commager and Richard B. Morris, eds., *The Spirit of Seventy-Six: The Story of the American Revolution as Told by Participants.* New York: Da Capo Press, 1995, p. 46.
14. Quoted in David Hackett Fischer, *Paul Revere's Ride.* New York: Oxford University Press, 1994, p. 6.
15. Quoted in Fischer, *Paul Revere's Ride,* p. 13.
16. Fischer, *Paul Revere's Ride,* p. 12.
17. Esther Forbes, *Paul Revere and the World He Lived In.* New York: Houghton Mifflin, 1942, p. 33.
18. Quoted in Jack P. Greene and J.R. Pole, *The Blackwell Encyclopedia of the American Revolution.* Malden, MA: Blackwell, 1991, p. 688.
19. Fred Anderson, *Crucible of War: The Seven Years' War and the Fate of Empire in British North America, 1754–1766.* New York: Vintage Books, 2000, pp. 139–40.
20. Fischer, *Paul Revere's Ride,* p. 22.

21. Quoted in Fischer, *Paul Revere's Ride*, pp. 25–26.
22. Quoted in Commager and Morris, *The Spirit of Seventy-Six*, pp. 66–67.
23. Quoted in Commager and Morris, *The Spirit of Seventy-Six*, p. 67.
24. Quoted in Commager and Morris, *The Spirit of Seventy-Six*, p. 67.
25. Quoted in Commager and Morris, *The Spirit of Seventy-Six*, p. 67.
26. Quoted in Commager and Morris, *The Spirit of Seventy-Six*, p. 68.
27. Quoted in Commager and Morris, *The Spirit of Seventy-Six*, p. 68.
28. Quoted in Commager and Morris, *To the Spirit of Seventy-Six*, p. 69.

Chapter 3: John Adams

29. Quoted in James Bishop Peabody, ed., *John Adams: A Biography in His Own Words*. New York: Newsweek, 1973, p. 20.
30. McCullough, *John Adams*, p. 47.
31. Quoted in L.H. Butterfield, Marc Friedlander, and Mary-Jo Kline, eds., *The Book of Abigail and John: Selected Letters of the Adams Family, 1762–1784*. Cambridge, MA: Harvard University Press, 1975, p. 19.
32. Quoted in Butterfield et al., *The Book of Abigail and John*, p. 51.
33. Quoted in McCullough, *John Adams*, pp. 60–61.
34. Quoted in Peabody, *John Adams*, pp. 116–17.
35. Quoted in Peabody, *John Adams*, p. 118.
36. Quoted in McCullough, *John Adams*, p. 67.
37. Quoted in Peabody, *John Adams*, p. 121.
38. Quoted in Butterfield et al., *The Book of Abigail and John*, p. 105.
39. Quoted in Butterfield et al., *The Book of Abigail and John*, p. 129.
40. John Ferling, *John Adams: A Life*. New York: Henry Holt, 1992, p. 147.
41. Quoted in Butterfield et al., *The Book of Abigail and John*, p. 139.
42. Quoted in Butterfield et al., *The Book of Abigail and John*, p. 140.
43. Quoted in Butterfield et al., *The Book of Abigail and John*, p. 142.
44. Quoted in Butterfield et al., *The Book of Abigail and John*, p. 215.
45. Constitution of the Commonwealth of Massachusetts, Ch. 5, sec. 2: The Encouragement of Literature, etc. www.state.ma.us.
46. McCullough, *John Adams*, p. 233.
47. Ferling, *John Adams*, p. 237.
48. Quoted in McCullough, *John Adams*, p. 447.
49. Quoted in Lester J. Cappon, ed., *The Adams-Jefferson Letters: The Complete Correspondence Between Thomas Jefferson and Abigail and John Adams*. Chapel Hill: University of North Carolina Press, 1959, p. 290.
50. Quoted in Ferling, *John Adams*, p. 444.

Chapter 4: Thomas Jefferson

51. Quoted in John Bartlett, *Familiar Quotations*, ed. Justin Kaplan. Boston: Little, Brown, 1992, p. 741.

52. Pauline Maier, ed., *The Declaration of Independence and the Constitution of the United States.* New York: Bantam Books, 1998, p. 53.

53. Fawn M. Brodie, *Thomas Jefferson: An Intimate History.* New York: W.W. Norton, 1974, p. 22.

54. Thomas Jefferson, *Writings,* ed. Merrill D. Peterson. New York: Library of America, 1984, p. 4.

55. Jefferson, *Writings,* p. 4.

56. Willard Sterne Randall, *Thomas Jefferson: A Life.* New York: Henry Holt, 1993, p. 57.

57. Brodie, *Thomas Jefferson,* p. 57.

58. Brodie, *Thomas Jefferson,* p. 61.

59. Jefferson, *Writings,* pp. 1,321–22.

60. Jefferson, *Writings,* pp. 5–6.

61. Jefferson, *Writings,* pp. 6–7.

62. Jefferson, *Writings,* p. 17.

63. Quoted in Randall, *Thomas Jefferson,* pp. 267–68.

64. Randall, *Thomas Jefferson,* p. 285.

65. Randall, *Thomas Jefferson,* p. 285.

66. Randall, *Thomas Jefferson,* p. 312.

67. Jefferson, *Writings,* pp. 1,516–17.

Chapter 5: Alexander Hamilton

68. Alexander Hamilton, *Writings,* ed. Joanne B. Freeman. New York: Library of America, 2001, p. 3.

69. Hamilton, *Writings,* p. 6.

70. Hamilton, *Writings,* p. 12.

71. Richard Brookhiser, *Alexander Hamilton, American.* New York: The Free Press, 1999, p. 26.

72. Noemie Emery, *Alexander Hamilton: An Intimate Portrait.* New York: G.P. Putnam's Sons, 1982, p. 35.

73. Emery, *Alexander Hamilton,* p. 37.

74. Broadus Mitchell, *Alexander Hamilton: A Concise Biography.* New York: Barnes & Noble, 1999, p. 48

75. Hamilton, *Writings,* p. 60.

76. Hamilton, *Writings,* p. 90.

77. Hamilton, *Writings,* p. 91.

78. Hamilton, *Writings,* pp. 93–94.

79. Hamilton, *Writings,* p. 895.

80. George Washington, *Writings,* ed. John Rhodehamel. New York: Library of America, 1997, p. 1013.

81. Hamilton, *Writings,* p. 66.

82. Mitchell, *Alexander Hamilton,* p. 376.

☆ For Further Reading ☆

Mark M. Boatner, III, *Encyclopedia of the American Revolution.* Mechanicsburg, PA: Stackpole Books, 1994. A standard one-volume reference on the Revolution.

H.W. Brands, *The First American: The Life and Times of Benjamin Franklin.* New York: Random House, 2000. A good recent biography.

Joseph J. Ellis, *Founding Brothers: The Revolutionary Generation.* New York: Knopf, 2001. A popular history focusing on the relationships among the founders, especially after the Revolutionary War.

James Thomas Flexner, *The Young Hamilton.* New York: Fordham University Press, 1997. A detailed look at Hamilton's life through the end of the Revolutionary War.

Annette Gordon-Reed. *Thomas Jefferson and Sally Hemings: An American Controversy.* Charlottesville: University Press of Virginia, 2000. A close look at the historical evidence about Jefferson and Hemings, with a new foreword commenting on the DNA evidence.

E.M. Halliday, *Understanding Thomas Jefferson.* New York: Perennial, 2001. A brief biography that attempts to make Jefferson's apparent contradictions more understandable.

Robert Middlekauff, *The Glorious Cause: The American Revolution, 1763–1789.* New York: Oxford University Press, 1982. A standard history of the Revolutionary era.

John Rhodehamel, ed., *The American Revolution: Writings from the War of Independence.* New York: Library of America, 2001. An excellent compilation of writings by those who took part in the war.

Gordon S. Wood, *The American Revolution: A History.* New York: Modern Library, 2002. A brief account of the Revolution by a leading historian.

★ Works Consulted ★

Books

Fred Anderson, *Crucible of War: The Seven Years' War and the Fate of Empire in British North America, 1754–1766*. New York: Vintage Books, 2000. A thorough history of the conflict that in many ways set the stage for the Revolution.

John Bartlett, *Familiar Quotations*, Ed. Justin Kaplan. Boston: Little, Brown, 1992. A standard source for quotations.

Fawn M. Brodie, *Thomas Jefferson: An Intimate History*. New York: W.W. Norton, 1974. A highly controversial biography because Brodie thought it likely that Jefferson had fathered Sally Hemings's children.

Richard Brookhiser, *Alexander Hamilton, American*. New York: The Free Press, 1999. A brief recent biography that shows the relevance of Hamilton's ideas to today's issues.

L.H. Butterfield, Marc Friedlander, and Mary-Jo Kline, eds., *The Book of Abigail and John: Selected Letters of the Adams Family, 1762–1784*. Cambridge, MA: Harvard University Press, 1975. A collection of correspondence that clearly shows the wit, wisdom, and intelligence of two remarkable Americans.

Lester J. Cappon, *The Adams-Jefferson Letters: The Complete Correspondence Between Thomas Jefferson and Abigail and John Adams*. Chapel Hill: University of North Carolina Press, 1959. The Adams-Jefferson correspondence, especially the letters that followed their reconciliation in 1812, has been called the greatest exchange of ideas in American history.

Henry Steele Commager and Richard B. Morris, eds., *The Spirit of Seventy-Six: The Story of the American Revolution as Told by Participants*. New York: Da Capo Press, 1995. A fascinating collection of writings.

Noemie Emery, *Alexander Hamilton: An Intimate Portrait*. New York: G.P. Putnam's Sons, 1982. An interesting and readable biography.

John Ferling, *John Adams: A Life*. New York: Henry Holt, 1992. A highly regarded biography that describes the times in which Adams lived.

David Hackett Fischer, *Paul Revere's Ride*. New York: Oxford University Press, 1994. A thorough account of Revere and his role in the early days of the Revolution, especially contrasting Revere with Thomas Gage, who was both the British commander in chief and the royal governor of Massachusetts.

Esther Forbes, *Paul Revere and the World He Lived In*. New York: Houghton Mifflin, 1942. One of the few full-length biographies of Revere, it includes much information about social life and customs in Revere's Boston.

Benjamin Franklin, *Autobiography, Poor Richard, and Later Writings*. Ed. J.A. Leo Lemay. New York: Library of America, 1997. An excellent collection of Franklin's published writings and correspondence.

Jack P. Greene and J.R. Pole, *The Blackwell Encyclopedia of the American Revolution*. Malden, MA: Blackwell, 1994. A scholarly overview of the Revolution and the issues that surrounded it.

Alexander Hamilton, *Writings*. Ed. Joanne B. Freeman. New York: Library of America, 2001. A representative collection of Hamilton's journalism, state papers, and correspondence.

Thomas Jefferson, *Writings*. Ed. Merrill D. Peterson. New York: Library of America, 1984. A good sampling of Jefferson's vast correspondence and his writings on science, agriculture, architecture, politics, and economics.

A.J. Langguth, *Patriots: The Men Who Started the American Revolution*. New York: Simon and Schuster, 1988. An excellent popular history of the Revolution.

Henry Wadsworth Longfellow, *Poems and Other Writings*. Ed. J.D. McClatchy. New York: Library of America, 2000. Longfellow's poem about Paul Revere's ride, while not historically accurate, brought Revere and the Battles of Lexington and Concord to the attention of the nation.

Pauline Maier, ed., *The Declaration of Independence and the Constitution of the United States*. New York: Bantam Books, 1998, p. 53.

David McCullough, *John Adams*. New York: Simon and Schuster, 2001. A very popular recent biography.

Broadus Mitchell, *Alexander Hamilton: A Concise Biography*. New York: Barnes & Noble, 1999. An abridgement of the author's two-volume biography of Hamilton, with a new introduction by historian Joanne B. Freeman.

James Bishop Peabody, ed., *John Adams: A Biography in His Own Words*. New York: Newsweek, 1973. A compilation of Adams's writings that includes helpful explanatory material.

Willard Sterne Randall, *Thomas Jefferson: A Life*. New York: Henry Holt, 1993. One of the standard biographies of Jefferson.

George Washington, *Writings*. Ed. John Rhodehamel. New York: Library of America, 1997. Though not thought of as a great writer, this collection shows the range of Washington's interests and ideas, mainly through his correspondence.

Esmond Wright, *Benjamin Franklin: His Life as He Wrote It*. Cambridge, MA: Harvard University Press, 1989. A life of Franklin that draws heavily on his *Autobiography* up to 1757 and then on his correspondence and journalism.

Internet Source

Constitution of the Commonwealth of Massachusetts, Ch. 5, sec. 2: The Encouragement of Literature, etc. www.state.ma.us.

★ Index ★

★ Picture Credits ★

Cover: Hulton/Archive by Getty Images

© Angelo Hornak/CORBIS, 78

© Bettmann/CORBIS, 15, 29, 33, 36

© Burstein Collection/CORBIS, 35

© CORBIS, 26, 59

Dover Publications, Inc., 10, 49, 74, 87

Hulton/Archive by Getty Images, 13, 18, 19, 32, 40, 46, 52, 62, 64, 68, 69, 82, 84, 92, 94, 97

Library of Congress, 21, 24, 34, 45, 47, 53, 71, 93

North Wind Picture Archives, 50, 63, 90

Steve Zmina, 42

☆ About the Author ☆

Charles Clark is a writer and editor who lives in Georgia.